I0474945

save give live

The 3 Principles to Achieving Financial Freedom

Mkemo London

save give live
The 3 Principles to Achieving Financial Freedom

Printed in the United States of America
First Edition

ISBN-13: 978-1456555139
ISBN-10: 1456555138

Contact Information:

Email: mkemo@dailypf.com
Website: www.dailypf.com

Connect on Social Media

Facebook.com/dailypf
Twitter.com/thedailypf
Instagram.com/dailypf

To my father Sammie,

I am a better man because of all the advice and wisdom you gave me as I journeyed into manhood. God rest your soul.

To my mother Cynthia,

Your guidance, wisdom and strength have been a constant inspiration throughout my life.

To my brother Sipho,

I have always appreciated and valued your friendship and compassion. You always believed in my countless business ideas and me.
I will always remember you.

To my sister Jewel,

Your faith and encouragement in all that I do has always been a beacon of light in my life.

Also available from Mkemo London:

Building Wealth with $50:
The 50 Best Dividend Stocks to Buy without a Broker

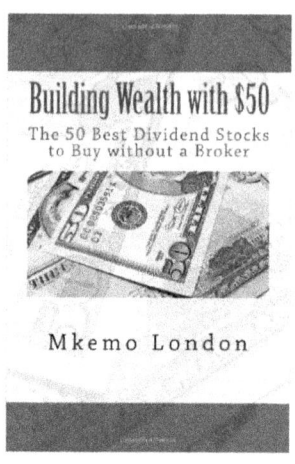

save give live
Workbook

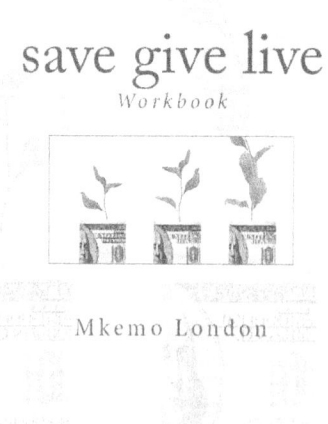

Coming Soon

Available wherever books are sold online.

CONTENTS

GIVE

Principle #2
Give your money to the things that bring value to your life.

LIVE

Principle #3
Live within your income.

Chapter 7
A Home for your Money

99

Chapter 8
The Money Plan

105

INTRODUCTION

My first encounter with earning money came when I was 12 years old. One Saturday morning after a major snowstorm, my younger brother and I ventured out into the bitter cold to shovel the snow off of our neighbor's sidewalks. During the course of the day we knocked on what seemed like dozens of doors to offer our snow removal services. We charged $10 per sidewalk and $5 per car. The Philadelphia winter of 1985 was especially harsh with temperatures in the low teens. Our gloves could barely keep our hands warm enough to hold the shovel and the wind just made it colder. The promise of financial gain and the satisfaction of a job well done motivated us through those blistering conditions to complete our work. By the end of the day we were both physically and mentally exhausted.

Deciding what to do with our newfound wealth was an endless topic of discussion. After we shared a couple slices of pizza from the local shop on the avenue, we divided the rest of the money evenly. We further discussed what we were going to purchase with the money that was burning a hole in our pockets. The top choices were between a pair of Doctor J Converse sneakers; we were huge Philadelphia 76ers fans, or a new video game for our Atari 2600 game console. However, our mother, who was always teaching us the value of a dollar, decided it was time we learned about saving money.

The next Saturday, my brother and I, accompanied our mother to the local bank to open savings accounts for each of us with the money we had earned from shoveling snow. Our mother believed that developing strong saving habits at an early age would benefit us later in life. This trip to the bank was my first opportunity to learn about how bank accounts worked.

Upon arriving at the bank, we were greeted by a tall man in a brown suit. After opening our savings accounts, he showed us how to fill out the deposit slips and proceeded to give us a lesson on compound interest. This is the process that allows your money to grow in the account from interest payments. He also informed us that our money would continue to grow if we made more deposits and didn't make withdrawals. But, we were still thinking about what we were going to purchase with the money we had worked so hard to earn. Our mother informed us that we were free to deposit and withdraw money, as we so desired. When we got outside my mother told us something that would stay with me to this day. She said, "Whatever you do with your money don't waste it, because you can only spend money once."

As a teenager, I spent my summers working for minimum wage. I did various jobs from cooking hamburgers to bagging groceries, all for the wage of $3.35 an hour. I can hardly believe that was the amount I earned, but it seemed like plenty of money at the time. Now, the federal minimum wage is $7.25, which isn't much of an increase compared to the cost of living today. Back then it was enough money for me to make the purchases I wanted. This included, adding to my cassette tape collection, going to the movies and eating Philly cheesesteaks with my friends. Those jobs taught me the value of hard work and the importance of getting up every day to earn my own money. Life was pretty simple back then. Throughout my years as a teenager, my parents were always advising me to save money and my grandmother Pauline would say, "Put your money in the bank, because you never know when you might need it for a rainy day". That was great advice. Although, I still had my savings account at the local bank, I had a feeling that there was more to money management than just earning, saving and spending money on the things I wanted.

At age 16, after my first summer job, I received my W-2 tax forms from my employer. This is the form that reported how much money I earned the previous summer. This was my introduction to the Internal Revenue Service. My mother helped me prepare my federal and state tax returns and I mailed them the next day. About six weeks later, I received just over $500 from my tax returns and I was absolutely thrilled. The experience of receiving that money affirmed that there was more to personal finance than what I knew.

Over the next 20 years, like most people, I would learn about credit, mortgages and budgeting from trial and error, and by making good and bad decisions. Today, both marriage and homeownership have taught me valuable lessons about maintaining the balance between what I want, with what I need, using the money I have. My journey to learn more about financial literacy continues every day.

Learning the basics of managing money can be a challenging task. Like anything else in life, you have to develop your money management skills with practice and building good habits. This book is about being proactive with your finances using the three principles: save, give, live. These three ground rules have been developed from my financial journey. I will discuss the concepts and strategies that have guided me to develop a strong financial foundation. I will also discuss the experiences that have helped me navigate the ups and downs of saving and managing money efficiently.

Save, give, live is divided into three principles:

- **Principle #1**: **Save your money for your tomorrow**. This concept is the foundation to building a strong financial future. Developing the habit of saving money for emergencies, retirement and making purchases is the main factor in limiting your debt. This will limit your need to use credit cards to borrow money. This is the first step towards financial freedom. Remember, every saved dollar you use to make purchases, is one less dollar you have to borrow.

- **Principle #2**: **Give your money to the things that bring value to your life**. Spending money on anything you want is the same as choosing to give your money to that item, experience or organization. When you spend your money on something make sure it enhances your life. When using credit to purchase a car, fund an education or purchase a home, it is important that you are getting real value for your money. You also have to protect yourself and your valuables by buying insurance.

- **Principle #3**: **Live within your income**. The concept of living within the income you currently have, is simply finding the balance between your expenses, spending money and saving money. This concept also determines how much debt you will manage in three major categories, which are your home, your car and your education. The most important factor to this principle is using a money plan and having a solid relationship with a financial institution to successfully live within your income.

INTRODUCTION

Managing money is a lot like driving a car. Before you start your journey, you have a destination you are trying to reach. When you are traveling, every turn or lane merge is done for a reason. Also, to reach your destination you have directions from a map or GPS device. Your approach to money should have the same precise purpose; there shouldn't be any decisions you make with your money that doesn't have a purpose or a plan. Similar to driving a car, when it comes to money management there are many variables that can throw you off your path. But, with the proper tools and money management skills, like a savings plan and a money plan, you can reach any destination you have for your money and your life.

The chapters in this book represent eight pillars of personal finance. They are your road map to setting up a strong financial life. Starting with savings and retirement then moving to credit, loans, home buying and insurance, ending with banking and the money plan or budgeting. These are the cornerstones and the individual topics that form the foundation for your financial freedom.

I have written this book for the everyday person trying to gain or regain freedom over their financial situation. This book is a guideline to point you in the right direction with common money questions and decisions. These are my experiences and stories. I hope they can help you with your financial concerns.

SAVE

Principle #1
Save your money for your tomorrow.

1

Pay Yourself First

"The starting point of all achievement is desire."

~Napoleon Hill

A few days after graduating from high school, I was with one of my friends; we were on our way to a suburban mall to purchase his mother a birthday gift. While at the mall we made a slight detour into the men's department at Macy's and into the Ralph Lauren section. Now, these were the clothes that were worn by the best dressed and most stylish people of our time, at least to us and was a true luxury brand. I browsed the sea of endless possibilities for an opportunity to make a purchase with the cash I had in my wallet. I suddenly saw this royal blue Ralph Lauren Polo Shirt, with white buttons and matching white logo with a button down collar and I just knew this garment was going home with me. I approached this symbol of upscale living and turned over the tag, only to discover the stark reality of luxury. The price was an alarming $100 for this shirt. What? That was a lot more than the $50 I had in my wallet for this purchase. I was disappointed, because I felt that luxury and all that it represented was out of my reach. On the ride back to the city, staring out of the rain soaked car window, I wondered to myself.

How would I ever be able to acquire such a symbol of opulence? At the time, I only worked full-time for the summer and was planning to attend college in the fall. My friend sensing my disappointment offered some advice that would start to change my entire perspective on affording luxury items. He said, "If you save $34 a week for three weeks you would have enough money for the shirt". It was like a light bulb went off and I had an "aha moment". It would be hard work saving money every week in pursuit of presenting a greater appearance to the world. But, I did it.

Adopting this simple concept allowed me to not only purchase the royal blue shirt, but I also amassed a wardrobe of name brand labels fit for my ascension into adulthood. My father Sam would often say, "Buy quality items, so you only have to spend money once." He was right. Many of these items would remain in my wardrobe for years. These purchases were my first possessions that made me feel like I was acquiring affluence, however small it might have been. Knowing I had saved my money to make this goal a reality, gave me a great feeling of accomplishment that washed over me as I made each purchase. I would later learn that you have to find a balance between acquiring luxury items and meeting your daily needs.

These possessions also allowed me, for the first time, to recognize how emotional and practical my relationship with money was going to be. The struggle to find that balance is at the heart of most financial decisions. What should I spend my money on? This is a question that I asked myself almost daily, even to this day.

It all started with learning and embracing the sacrifice and discipline it takes to save money for the things I wanted. Saving money is not easy. However, my first savings account taught me the value of saving money to reach a goal. Learning that lesson opened my eyes to the benefits of having discipline and working hard to reach freedom with a financial situation. The action of putting money away for the things in my life that I wanted was the first step towards claiming independence from relying on borrowing money for my every desire. It does not matter how much money you make, you have to be dedicated to saving some of it. In order to do that, I learned you must pay yourself first.

The easiest way to start saving money is to have it automatically deducted from your checking account or your paycheck using direct deposit into a savings account. Sending a set amount of money to your savings account every time you receive a paycheck is a strategy that will help your savings accumulate quickly. This strategy will also provide you with the money you need for both emergencies and when you want to treat yourself to something nice.

There are **two accounts** that you need to have on your journey to saving money. They are the ME Fund and a SAFE Fund.

The ME Fund

The ME fund which stands for "My Everything", is the money that you spend on things that bring you happiness, whether it's an item or an experience with friends or family. Put money into this savings account before you pay anything else. This account should be set up at a financial institution that is separate from your main checking account. That will make it harder to access the money for everyday expenses. We are all working for more than just surviving and paying bills. Creating a fund for the items you want instead of taking the money from your living expenses is the purpose of this account.

How much should you put in this account? The amount you select is your choice. However, you could try to start saving at least $25 per week. The following chart shows how quickly this small amount adds up to $500 in just five months and this is without any bank interest.

Time	Amount	Total
Week 1	$25.00	$25.00
Week 2	$25.00	$50.00
Week 3	$25.00	$75.00
Week 4	$25.00	$100.00
Week 5	$25.00	$125.00
Week 6	$25.00	$150.00
Week 7	$25.00	$175.00
Week 8	$25.00	$200.00
Week 9	$25.00	$225.00
Week 10	$25.00	$250.00
Week 11	$25.00	$275.00
Week 12	$25.00	$300.00
Week 13	$25.00	$325.00
Week 14	$25.00	$350.00
Week 15	$25.00	$375.00
Week 16	$25.00	$400.00
Week 17	$25.00	$425.00
Week 18	$25.00	$450.00
Week 19	$25.00	$475.00
Week 20	$25.00	$500.00

Establishing a ME fund is a necessary step to getting the things you enjoy, while maintaining a realistic balance between the things you need, with the things you want, using the money you have.

The SAFE Fund

The SAFE fund, which stands for "Saving Amounts For Emergencies", will provide a financial cushion in the event a crisis or an unforeseen circumstance presents itself. Having money set aside for an unexpected car repair, home repair or job loss, is a necessary step in your financial life. This fund is designed to prepare you for a situation that is out of the ordinary. Experts recommend having three to six months of income or living expenses in this fund. However, each person and family is different. The most important thing to remember about this fund is to start it as soon as possible or if you have one, continue to add money to it. The alterative to a SAFE fund would be to borrow money using credit cards or from friends and family. Those options should only be used as a last resort. The amount you need in this fund is based on your own needs and circumstances. Similar to your ME fund, this account should also be set up at a financial institution that is separate from your main checking account. Having a goal to work towards like saving $1,000 is a good place to start. Saving $1,000 may sound like a lot of money, but this goal can be achieved by either saving every week automatically from your checking account or by following the 52-week saving challenge.

The 52-Week Saving Challenge

This challenge has been seen on the Internet in recent years, but I have made a slight change to it. This challenge will allow you to save over $1,300 in one year.

The 52-Week Saving Challenge

Time	Amount	Total	Time	Amount	Total
Week 1	$1.00	$1.00	Week 27	$14.00	$703.00
Week 2	$52.00	$53.00	Week 28	$39.00	$742.00
Week 3	$2.00	$55.00	Week 29	$15.00	$757.00
Week 4	$51.00	$106.00	Week 30	$38.00	$795.00
Week 5	$3.00	$109.00	Week 31	$16.00	$811.00
Week 6	$50.00	$159.00	Week 32	$37.00	$848.00
Week 7	$4.00	$163.00	Week 33	$17.00	$865.00
Week 8	$49.00	$212.00	Week 34	$36.00	$901.00
Week 9	$5.00	$217.00	Week 35	$18.00	$919.00
Week 10	$48.00	$265.00	Week 36	$35.00	$954.00
Week 11	$6.00	$271.00	Week 37	$19.00	$973.00
Week 12	$47.00	$318.00	Week 38	$34.00	$1,007.00
Week 13	$7.00	$325.00	Week 39	$20.00	$1,027.00
Week 14	$46.00	$371.00	Week 40	$33.00	$1,060.00
Week 15	$8.00	$379.00	Week 41	$21.00	$1,081.00
Week 16	$45.00	$424.00	Week 42	$32.00	$1,113.00
Week 17	$9.00	$433.00	Week 43	$22.00	$1,135.00
Week 18	$44.00	$477.00	Week 44	$31.00	$1,166.00
Week 19	$10.00	$487.00	Week 45	$23.00	$1,189.00
Week 20	$43.00	$530.00	Week 46	$30.00	$1,219.00
Week 21	$11.00	$541.00	Week 47	$24.00	$1,243.00
Week 22	$42.00	$583.00	Week 48	$29.00	$1,272.00
Week 23	$12.00	$595.00	Week 49	$25.00	$1,297.00
Week 24	$41.00	$636.00	Week 50	$28.00	$1,325.00
Week 25	$13.00	$649.00	Week 51	$26.00	$1,351.00
Week 26	$40.00	$689.00	Week 52	$27.00	*$1,378.00*

Every week, transfer a different dollar amount from your checking account according to the week on the chart. For instance, Week 1 transfer $1 into the account, the next week transfer $52 and so on. This is a savings schedule that allows your funds to accumulate without putting a burden on you at the end of the year when holiday spending becomes a priority.

Short Term Savings

There are three options for where to save money for the ME fund and the SAFE fund, not including an envelope in your sock drawer.

Traditional Banks

Using a traditional bank for these two funds has the advantage (or possibly disadvantage) of multiple locations, which will allow you the convenience to access your money with ease. However, remember that the easier it is to get to your funds, the easier it will be to spend the money versus saving it. Also, the Federal Deposit Insurance Corporation (FDIC) insures the account. The FDIC is a government agency that will protect your money up to $250,000; this agency insures that your money is safe from bank failure. The interest at banks may be small, but it will still help your savings grow. At traditional banks, please be aware of the fees associated with savings accounts, like minimum daily balance requirements. The initial deposit amount for this type of account is usually $100.

Credit Unions

A credit union is like a bank, but they are set up as a non-profit. It takes a little research to find out if you are eligible to join a credit union. They offer similar interest rates as banks, but they have lower fees on savings accounts. One advantage to most credit unions is they usually have fewer locations than traditional banks, so this may help you to not touch the money. The National Credit Union Administration (NCUA) is an agency that will protect your money up to $250,000, just like the FDIC. Credit unions are a good option for your two funds, mainly because of the low fees associated with savings accounts and the initial deposit amount can be as low as $5.

Online Banks

Using online banks has become popular in recent years. Online savings accounts offer higher interest rates, because they operate online and don't have the costs that a traditional bank or credit union may have, such as paying for locations. For example, banks similar to Ally Financial and Capital One 360 are good places to start looking into a savings account online. The FDIC also insures these accounts and the initial deposit amount can also be as low as $5. You can go to **www.bankrate.com** and compare online banks to find the one that suits your needs.

Long Term Savings

Certificate of Deposit (CD)

Finally, another way to put savings into your financial plan is a certificate of deposit. A certificate of deposit is not a physical piece of paper issued by a bank or credit union. A certificate of deposit is a financial instrument that locks in your money for a set period of time, usually between three months and five years. In exchange for keeping your money for this time period, you will receive a fixed amount of interest. The longer the time period the more interest you will earn.

A certificate of deposit offers more interest than a savings account because you are promising not to touch your money for the agreed amount of time. The interest is usually paid at the end of the period when the CD "matures".

The best place to investigate this long term savings instrument is at the financial institution where you currently have your main checking account. The Federal Deposit Insurance Corporation (FDIC) and the National Credit Union Administration (NCUA) also insure certificates of deposit up to $250,000.

When comparing the interest rates of various CDs, it is important to understand the difference between annual percentage yield (APY) and annual percentage rate (APR). APY is the total amount of interest the CD will earn in one year, taking compound interest into account. APR is the stated interest rate earned in one year, without taking compound interest into account.

For example, John deposits $1,000 into a 1 year CD that pays a 5% APR semiannually (every 6 months). He will receive an interest payment of $25 after the first 6 months ($1,000 x .05 x .5 years). The $25 is added to the $1,000 for a total of $1,025 and the CD continues to earn 5% interest for the remainder of the year. At the end of the next 6 months the interest is $25.63 ($1,025 x .05 x .5 years) for a total of $1,050.63 for the entire year. The APY is $50.63, because of the compound interest. Compound interest adds up when both the principle and interest continue to earn more interest over time.

A certificate of deposit has fees or penalties for early withdrawals before the maturity date. Penalty fees usually keep investors from withdrawing their money from the CD before the agreed upon date. Typically, financial institutions will charge you a set amount of interest as a penalty for early withdrawals from a CD, but you will receive all of your original investment. You should make every effort to keep your money in the CD until it matures.

Where would you get the money to put into a CD? A good source for finding money to put in a CD can be as simple as saving a portion of your annual federal or state tax refund check. For instance, if you get your refund check in February and you invest $500 in a 9 month CD that matures in November, you will have money for the holidays with interest. You could also leave the money in the CD for an additional 9 months or change it to a 1-year CD and continue to earn more interest.

Establishing a ME Fund, SAFE Fund and investing in CDs are good accounts to have on your road to saving for emergencies and the things you want. Much like when I saved my money for that Ralph Lauren shirt. Remember, every saved dollar you use for purchases, is one less dollar you have to borrow. I have recommended specific amounts to start your savings plans. But, even if you save $5 a week it is a good start, as long as you continue saving. Remember, the money in each fund is used to take care of situations that otherwise some people would consider using credit cards.

Saving money is a habit that has to be developed early in life using hard work, discipline and focus. When you earn money, you must save money to have money. This is freedom. Having money saved is freedom from borrowing, freedom from worrying, freedom from the unknown. When you have money saved you have choices and having choices is what life is all about.

2

You Can't Work Forever

"A year from now you may wish you started today"

~*Karen Lamb*

When I was a teenager, my mother worked for a small non-profit organization in the heart of North Philadelphia. She loved that job. Working with children and helping people had been her life's mission and she had reached that rare feeling of fulfillment at her place of employment. This organization not only provided early childhood educational services for young children, it was a real pillar of strength in the community. However, this job offered very little in the area of pay and benefits. One benefit they did offer was a 403(b) retirement plan. A 403(b) retirement plan is set up for non-profit employees to invest their money in mutual funds that earn interest and are a way for people to have money when they retire. This plan is similar to a 401(k) plan offered by for profit corporations.

Many employees at this organization were hesitant to participant in this retirement plan, including my mother. In those days many people still believed that having a pension or defined benefit was the only plan that would provide you with income in retirement. A pension is a plan that provides guaranteed income in retirement based on your salary regardless of the amount the employee contributes. There was just one small problem; this organization didn't have a pension plan. One day, a presentation was made to the employees to inform them that they had to join the 403(b) plan, otherwise they wouldn't have any money for retirement other than social security. My mother and her fellow co-workers were not accustomed to the idea of having to save for their own retirement. It was a new day. My mother started contributing a small amount of her bi-weekly salary to the 403(b) plan. At the end of every year the organization would contribute a set dollar amount to all the employees that participated in the plan. This type of retirement plan provides a lump sum of money when the employee reaches retirement age which is usually around 60 years old. The 403(b) plan and social security would be all the retirement income my mother would have to rely on when she retired.

One year, due to an unforeseen hardship my mother had to withdraw all the money she had saved in the 403(b) retirement plan. She was very disappointed and discouraged with the idea of having to start over with saving for her retirement. During this time she returned to college to complete her education. Upon completing her associate degree from the local community college, my mother decided it was time for a change. With very little saved for retirement, she knew she had to find a job that offered a defined benefit plan or pension. The thought of leaving the job that she loved for so many years was a terrifying notion.

At this point my siblings and I were all teenagers and she felt that it was time to muster up the courage to make the change. After a few months of interviewing, my mother received a job offer from a company, which provided a defined benefit plan or pension to all of its employees. She was thrilled. Starting a new job with a new company after 16 years of working for the same organization was a very difficult decision. However, she knew she had to prepare for her retirement.

After working 26 years on her new job, my mother retired and loves it. With social security, the pension and some savings, she has been able to enjoy a comfortable retirement. We should all be so fortunate.

Getting started with Savings for Retirement

Why talk about retirement in the second chapter of this book? Creating a solid retirement savings plan is too important not to start as early as possible. Starting retirement savings early will provide you with the maximum amount of time to grow your money.

Unlike my mother, most people will not have a pension to rely on for retirement income. A pension is a benefit that is becoming a thing of the past much like the DVD player and compact discs; they are going away for the American worker. Most people will only have a combination of social security, a 401(k)/403(b) retirement plan and an individual retirement account (IRA), to rely on when the time comes to retire from the workforce. Will these accounts be enough? Let's find out.

Social Security

Social security is currently the main source of income for the average working person in America when they retire. Social security is a retirement benefit provided by the United States government. Almost every worker in America pays into the social security program. In 2016, workers pay 6.2% of their earnings from each paycheck into the social security system through payroll taxes on earnings up to $118,500. Your employer pays an additional 6.2% on your behalf. Entrepreneurs must pay the full 12.4% of their income towards social security.

When you retire the government issues you a benefit check based on the total amount of money you and your employers paid into the social security system. The social security benefit payments are calculated based on your highest earning 35 years in the workforce. The government knows that you earn more money the older you get and with that in mind, most people's benefit will be based on their work history from age 30 to age 65. If you haven't worked 35 years, those non-working years are counted as a 0 for the calculation. As long as you have worked at least a minimum of 10 years at a minimum wage job, that deducted the social security tax out of your paycheck, you are eligible for the benefit.

When you reach full retirement age you are eligible to start collecting your social security benefit. Full retirement age is based on when you were born. If you were born between 1943 and 1954 full retirement is age 66, if you were born between 1955 and 1960 the age varies between 66 and 67. If you were born in 1960 or later your full retirement age is 67.

Some people don't wait until full retirement age and are able to start collecting benefits at age 62, however they will receive a slightly reduced payment. On the other hand, if you work past your full retirement age your payment will increase 8% per year to age 70. It is recommended that you wait until full retirement age to start receiving your benefits.

Remember, you are replacing your income from your employment and you may need to receive as much money as you can to have a decent amount of income in retirement. If you are married, your spouse should also wait until full retirement age to start receiving benefits. The two incomes will add up to an income that is higher than if you both elected to receive benefits sooner.

The following chart displays the amounts you would receive if you were entitled to $1,341 a month, which is the average amount currently being issued to retirees today at full retirement age. This is compared to the amount you would receive if you elected to start receiving benefits at age 62. This chart accounts for the population that will be eligible for benefits in the coming years.

Full Retirement Age versus Age 62 Benefit by Year of Birth

		At Age 62	
Year of Birth	Full Retirement Age	A $1,341 Retirement Benefit would be reduced to	The retirement benefit is reduced by this %
1943-1954	66	$1,005.75	25.00%
1955	66 and 2 months	$994.61	25.83%
1956	66 and 4 months	$983.35	26.67%
1957	66 and 6 months	$972.22	27.50%
1958	66 and 8 months	$961.09	28.33%
1959	66 and 10 months	$949.83	29.17%
1960 and later	67	$938.70	30.00%

Despite the current political climate in America, social security will be around for the next generation. Hopefully, it will remain in its current form. Only time will tell. For more information about how social security works visit the Social Security Administration's website at **www.ssa.gov**. You can sign up for an account and use the calculator on the website to figure out how much your estimated social security check will be when you retire.

As previously stated, the average social security monthly benefit is about $1,341 per month, for people who start collecting benefits at full retirement age. This level of income is not enough money to live on in retirement for the average working person in America, regardless of their current lifestyle. With that in mind, the U.S. government created two additional accounts to help people save for retirement, 401(k)/403(b) retirement plans and an Individual Retirement Account (IRA).

401(k) Retirement Plans

The 401(k) retirement plan is the next main source of income the average person can count on in retirement after social security. 401(k) plans are a pre-tax investment account that takes money out of each paycheck to contribute to mutual funds that are invested tax-free. Tax-free means you don't have to pay taxes on the interest you earn in your account. The maximum contribution amount for 2016 is $18,000 per year and if you are age 50 or older, you are able to contribute an additional $6,000 per year. This plan is the only retirement benefit offered by most employers. This plan also allows your money to grow tax-free until you withdraw it after you are age 59 ½ and when you are no longer employed at the company. When you start a new job, you should make it a priority to enroll in the

401(k) plan as soon as you are eligible or if you are working and have not signed up you should do so immediately. There are certain companies that administer retirement plans through your employer such as, Vanguard, Fidelity and Prudential.

How much should you Save in your 401(k)?

How much money you contribute to your 401(k) plan is up to you, it's your choice. Employers will usually allow each employee to either contribute a set dollar amount or a percentage of each paycheck into the plan. You may want to start with at least 4% of your pre-tax income. For example, if you earn $1,500 every two weeks and your contribution is 4%, the amount coming out of your check is just $60! The $60 gets deposited into your retirement account before taxes are taken out. Which means that you won't pay federal taxes on the $60. The following chart displays an example of how quickly this contribution will accumulate at just 6% interest; the interest is applied every month. No matter when you start saving for retirement, the contributions will add up as long as you keep money going into the plan. This chart does not include a match an employer may offer.

$60 Bi-weekly at a rate of 6%
interest compounded monthly

5 Years	$9,071.45
10 Years	$21,306.13
15 Years	$37,808.89
20 Years	$60,068.63
25 Years	$90,093.68
30 Years	$130,592.98

Employers Match

Some employers will match your contribution up to a certain percentage. For example, they may contribute an additional $.50 for every dollar you contribute, usually up to 50% of your contribution.

For example, if you contribute 4% or $60 of your $1,500 bi-weekly salary, the match may be 2% or $30. Remember the match is free money and the additional money will help your savings balance increase over time. At the very least, you should start your contributions with 2% of your pre-tax income. The following chart displays how quickly your contributions and the employers match will accumulate at just 6% interest; the interest is applied every month. This example does not include raises and promotions you might receive during your career.

$90 Bi-weekly at a rate of 6%
interest compounded monthly

5 Years	$13,606.50
10 Years	$31,958.29
15 Years	$56,712.10
20 Years	$90,101.28
25 Years	$135,138.29
30 Years	$195,886.46

Whether your employer matches your contributions or not, you should always make it a priority to invest in the 401(k) plan. In the 21st century saving for retirement is not optional. You have to save for retirement no matter what. Any size contribution will add up over time and will be a financial supplement to social security.

If you haven't started saving for retirement there is still time to start. It's never too late to start saving for your future. Developing this part of your financial plan has to start as soon as possible and is essential to having a secure retirement.

What are the Investment Options for 401(k) Plans?

Now that you have contributions being withdrawn from each paycheck, where should you invest your money for maximum and long-term returns? Many people are hesitant to invest in the 401(k) plan provided by their employer because the investment options are confusing and not explained in a simple fashion. The human resource departments at most jobs are not comfortable lending any advice towards investment decisions or explaining the options. They will tell you to call the investment company or advise you to do your own research. That can be challenging to the average person.

This is the information that is not normally explained and really doesn't exist in one place. Although, it is a lot of information and can be daunting, I am going to take you step by step highlighting the important pieces to know as you begin this part of your journey.

There are three things you need to be aware of before you fill out your 401(k) investment form.

1. Don't have more than 15% of your contributions going into one individual mutual fund. This simply means you want to diversify your account by choosing between the four major investment categories of stocks, bonds, blended and money market funds. If one investment is not doing well you won't have all of your money in that investment. Keeping your

money spread across these investment options over the course of your work life is a common strategy to follow.

2. Be aware of the fees that your plan is charging. There is a management fee associated with all 401(k) plans. These fees are commonly known as 12b-1 fees, which are charged either annually or quarterly. These fees are charged for managing all the investments in your account.

3. If you are under age 40, you should invest more in stocks than the other categories. You have many years until you reach retirement age. You will be able to take advantage of the gain stocks have over the long term.

As mentioned earlier the four main categories of investments to choose from within a 401(k) retirement plan are stock mutual funds, bond mutual funds, blended mutual funds and money market mutual funds. There are only mutual fund choices available in 401(k) plans. First, let's answer the main question most people have. What is a mutual fund?

Mutual Funds

A mutual fund is a professionally managed investment company that collects money from many people to invest in stocks or bonds. A manager charges a fee to each investor for buying and selling stocks and bonds for the investors. Much like buying a ticket to a concert, a ticket agent will charge you a fee for selling you the ticket to a show. The ticket agent keeps the fee whether you enjoyed the show or not. Just like a mutual fund manager will keep his fee whether you make money or not.

For example, four people who invest in the 401(k) have $35 withdrawn from each paycheck and invested into the U.S. Growth Fund, a large growth stock mutual fund. This means that all the stocks in the fund are from large stable American companies with the ability to make money and grow their business for investors. The mutual fund manager invests the total $140 ($35x4) into publicly traded American companies such as Coca-Cola, General Electric and American Express. Starting with 1 share of Coca-Cola (KO) at $50, 1 share of General Electric (GE) at $30 and 1 share of American Express (AXP) at $60 for a total of $140. Each investor does not own a piece of each company directly, but rather a share of the mutual fund. The mutual fund price is made up of the total number of shares divided by the total value of all the stocks in the portfolio; this is called the Net Asset Value (NAV). This chart illustrates what has been outlined above.

Company	Symbol	Shares	Price	Market Value
Coca- Cola	KO	1	$50.00	$50.00
American Express	AXP	1	$60.00	$60.00
General Electric	GE	1	$30.00	$30.00
				$140.00

The **3** shares are divided by the total market value of all the stocks, which is **$140** and distributed to each investor according to their contribution. ($140/3=$46.67)

Each investor owns a fractional share of the mutual fund, which is: ($35/$46.67 = .7466).

The following is an example of what your 401(k) statement will look like with the stock mutual fund investment from the example.

Mutual Fund	Quantity	NAV	Balance
U.S Growth Fund	.7499	$46.67	$35.00

Stock Mutual Funds

Stock mutual funds are divided into three main categories: Index, Growth and Value funds. (Note: I used a growth stock mutual fund in the previous example). Index funds invest in the publicly traded companies of an actual index. An Index is a collection of publicly traded companies that are in a particular segment of the stock market and they are monitored together to get a measurement of this part of the stock market, (i.e., utilities, transportation, healthcare, etc.). When an investor purchases a share of an index fund, he or she is purchasing a share of a portfolio that contains the securities in a particular index. The most popular of the index mutual funds in a 401(k) plan is the S&P 500. This fund is made up of the 500 largest publicly traded companies in the United States, like Exxon Mobile, Wal-Mart and Coca-Cola. Most 401(k) plans offer a version of this fund.

Also, there are stock mutual funds that invest primarily in U.S. companies that follow other stock market indexes such as the Nasdaq 100, which are the 100 largest companies on the Nasdaq such as Apple, Microsoft and Amazon. Growth and value funds invest in companies that are stable with strong records of paying dividends and being profitable, such as General Electric, Verizon and Nike. These stock funds are the most popular in a 401(k) plan and for good reason; they can represent some of the biggest gains in your retirement account. The younger you are the more time you have to invest in stock funds. Historically, U.S. stocks have a higher rate of return on investment than bonds and money market funds.

Stock funds have more risk associated with them; however, when you are investing for the long term, stock funds will provide steady growth and dividends. It is recommended that at least 70% of your contributions should be in stock funds if you are under age 30.

Bond Mutual Funds

Sometimes local, state and the federal government need to borrow money to finance specific projects, like bridges, schools and highways. Likewise companies need to expand their business operations and make purchases. In both cases bonds are issued. When you buy a bond, you are loaning your money for a certain period of time to a particular entity. In exchange, the entity pays you interest instead of dividends when the bond matures. Also, in the case of companies, bonds allow them to raise money without selling ownership in the company by issuing stock. Bond funds have less risk than stock funds. They also tend to be safer investments, like U.S. government bonds and corporate bonds of large U.S. corporations. Some of the major bond fund categories in a 401(k) plan are U.S. Treasury bonds, municipal bonds, corporate bonds and international bond funds and sometimes the bond funds are a combination of the many different categories. It is recommended that a portion of your 401(k) contribution be invested in bond funds.

Blended Mutual Funds

A blended fund is a combination of stocks and bonds in one portfolio. Generally, these hybrid funds tend to invest in a certain type of stock or bond. For instance, the fund could invest in dividend stocks and corporate bonds or value stocks and U.S treasury bonds. The fund usually sticks to a predetermined investment strategy that is directed towards the highest returns. It is recommended that a portion of your 401(k) contributions be invested in blended funds.

Money Market Mutual Funds

A money market mutual fund invests in short term, low risk debt securities such as U.S. Treasury bills and certificates of deposit. Primarily money market funds invest in very safe securities and offer the lowest return on your investment. These funds are able to pay interest to investors, which is reinvested into more shares of the fund. It is the absolute safest investment available; however it has a lower return on your money than stocks or bonds. If you are closer to retirement age, money market funds offer more safety than growth for your money.

When are you fully Vested in your 401(k)?

Your contributions and the employers match are fully invested and growing in the account. Being vested is when you get to keep the money that is in the account when you leave the company. The employers match is usually yours to keep after you have been employed and in the plan for a set number of years. Your contributions are 100% vested immediately.

401(k) Loans

Sometimes you need to borrow money for an event in your life that is not covered by your SAFE Fund. Your 401(k) retirement account offers low interest rates and no credit check. This option should always be viewed as a last resort. However, it is an easy option to access money for a real emergency.

Taking a loan through the 401(k) retirement plan means you're borrowing a portion of the money in your account and paying yourself back. When your vested balance in your 401(k) account reaches $2,000, you can borrow 50% of the balance, a minimum of $1,000, and up to a maximum of $50,000. You are required to repay the loan within five years. The repayment schedule may be extended if you're using the money for a down payment on a home. The interest rate on this loan is usually between 4% and 6%. There are good reasons to borrow money from your 401(k) like a down payment on a house or major home repair. Don't borrow money for a vacation or to make any purchase that could be achieved by saving money in your ME fund. Be aware of taking a 401(k) loan to pay credit card debt at a lower interest rate. There is too great a chance those same cards will be charged right back up again. Keep in mind that the loan comes directly out of your account; meaning they will sell funds from your 401(k) account to take the loan. Therefore, you are missing out on growth towards retirement income. Also, when you leave your job before age 59½, and you have a loan balance, you must repay the entire loan within 60 days or you will incur a 10% penalty and the balance will count towards earned income at tax time. During the repayment period it is important to keep your contributions as close to the same amount as possible, so that you keep receiving the same company match.

Rollovers

You may not work on the same job forever. When you leave your current employer, if you are not 59½ you will have to make a decision on what to do with the money in your 401(k). You will have four main options for your money.

1. **Keep it where it is.** Your first choice is to let your 401(k) plan stay at the investment company where it is currently invested. There may be a minimum amount to keep the account open. If the investments are making money and you like the funds offered in the plan, it may be best to stay invested in the plan. If you have more than one 401(k) plan from multiple jobs, it may become difficult to keep track of your retirement dollars.

2. **Cash it out.** This is an option that is available to you; it is by far the worse choice. You will receive the cash value of your account. However, you will have to pay state and federal taxes on the withdrawn cash, as well as a 10% penalty at tax time.

3. **Roll it into the new employer's plan.** Your new employer's human resources department will provide you with the instructions to move your old 401(k) into their plan. This will keep all your retirement plans in one place and managed by a professional manager.

4. **Open an Individual Retirement Account (IRA).** An IRA is a tax-deferred account that provides you the most investment options. All the dividends and capital gains that you receive are tax-free. IRAs allows you to access all of the mutual funds, individual stocks and bonds and the contributions may be tax deductible.

Individual Retirement Account

Rolling your 401(k) into this tax free account will allow you to completely manage your own retirement savings. You have the option to invest in mutual funds similar to your old 401(k) and you will have more information about the fees. If your employer doesn't offer a 401(k) plan or any other retirement plan, open an IRA to continue saving for retirement. There are two different versions of this account, which are traditional, and Roth.

Traditional IRA

The main features of traditional IRAs are your contributions can be deducted from your federal taxable income depending on your tax bracket. You are allowed to contribute up to $5,500 per year and $6,500 per year if you're over age 50. Most important when you reach retirement age and start making withdrawals, the cash will be taxed as regular income with no additional fees after you are 59½. For withdrawals before age 59½ there is a 10% tax and it is counted as regular income. IRAs give you access to all of the mutual funds, individual stocks, CDs and all types of bonds. You are able to have a mix of dividend paying stocks like Microsoft (MSFT), General Electric (GE) and American Express (AXP), as well as a variety of Index funds and bond funds. Most accounts can be open for as little as $20 and you are able to trade stocks and mutual funds for a low fee. It is in your best interest to investigate this option for a 401(k) rollover and as an additional savings for your retirement.

Roth IRA

The difference between the traditional IRA and a Roth IRA is the tax treatment. Roth IRA contributions are not tax deductible. Your money still grows tax free, meaning all the dividend and capital gains are not taxed. All withdrawals are also tax free. If you convert a traditional IRA to a Roth IRA you must wait five years to make any withdrawals without penalty. However, you are saving for retirement, you should not make any withdrawals until you retire.

Income after you Retire

Social security, 401(k) and IRA savings are the accounts the average American will have to rely on for income in retirement. After you retire, your 401(k) account and your IRA account will hold a sizeable amount of money, such as $100,000 or more. There is a rule of thumb about how much money you should withdraw every year from these accounts, called the 4% rule.

4% Rule

The 4% rule simply says, you should withdraw 4% of the total money you have saved in your 401(k) plan and IRA accounts every year to live. The 4% rule is only a guideline, you are able to withdraw more money if you need it, but remember this is the money you have to live on for all your retirement years. This money has to last.

All of your accounts and social security will amount to monthly income. The following example will illustrate how much money you could have.

For example, if you are retiring in 2016 and you are age 62, your social security check could be about $1,005. You have $210,000 in your 401(k) account and $150,000 in your IRA account. If you withdraw 4% each year out of each account, that would be $14,400 per year. Both social security and withdrawals from retirement accounts will be $2,205 per month.

Retirement Monthly Income

Social Security	$1,005
401(k)	$700
IRA	$500
Total Per Month	**$2,205**

Preparing for retirement is not easy. The one thing stopping many people from retirement is fear of not being prepared. The right decisions have to be made early in your career. This preparation comes with hard work and planning. When you reach retirement age, how do you want to live? Saving as much money as possible, as soon as possible, is the key to a comfortable retirement. Remember, the more money you invest, over the longest period of time will determine the money you have, for the life you want.

The principle of saving for your tomorrow, allows you to plan for events and situations in your life using discipline and your own money. From small items to retirement, developing a habit of savings will give you more opportunities and choices in your life.

GIVE

Principle #2
Give your money to the things that bring
value to your life.

3

Pay the $20

"The triumph can't be had without the struggle."

~ *Wilma Rudolph*

On my first day attending the Community College of Philadelphia, I was at the student activity center, and I came across a table giving away water bottles and notebooks. The only requirement to get this free notebook was to sign up for a Visa credit card. I thought ok, I could really use a free notebook and I am never going to get approved for a credit card, because I have no credit history. A few weeks later, to my utter surprise, I received a shiny new Visa credit card in the mail. It was silver with a blue logo and had my name in bold letters. This credit card was more than just another symbol of my ascension into adulthood; it was freedom. With a $600 credit limit, I was set!

According to the letter I received with the credit card, as a college student, I had the potential for future earnings. This would allow me to pay this credit card in full one day. When I first received this credit card, I honestly thought it was free money. I immediately went out and bought a new Sony Walkman, a pair of headphones and of course more Ralph Lauren clothing items. My thought at the time was that I didn't have to save anymore for the things I wanted. I could just use this credit card to make any purchase I wanted. A few weeks later, I received my first bill. Even though I had spent $510 of the $600 limit, I only had to make a $20 payment. I was relieved. I was worried that I had to pay the entire balance at once. At the time, I didn't have a checking account. So, I purchased a $20 money order from the U.S. post office and put the payment in the mail. Soon, I would have $110 on the card ($90+$20 payment). But, what I didn't factor in was the interest that was accruing on the balance at a rate of 25%. Well, when the next bill arrived, the available credit on the card had dwindled down to just $3. Between more purchases and the high interest rate, I had reached the credit limit. But, the minimum amount due was still only $20! Just over 3% of the balance.

Despite the fact that I paid the minimum payment of $20 every month, the balance never seemed to get any smaller due to the 25% interest rate accruing on the balance. As a result, I begin to become uninterested in paying my credit card bill. At the time I didn't fully understand the consequences this change in behavior was going to have on my credit. There were many times I had to make a choice between paying this bill and having some money in my pocket. I chose the spending money option far too often. A few months later, I received a letter from Visa informing me that my credit card was cancelled. I was very disappointed. My beginning steps on the road to financial independence just took a sharp turn into a ditch. I had acquired credit and was entrusted with the responsibility of its management and now it was lost. How could my credit card be cancelled? I still owed a balance. So, let me get this straight, I could no longer use the card, it was still incurring 25% interest and I still had to pay the balance?

How was that fair? If I had just continued to pay the $20, the credit card wouldn't have been cancelled.

It took me over a year to pay that credit card off. I didn't get another card for three years. The lesson I learned from that experience was not that debt was a terrible burden or paying credit card interest is wasted money but, that I should use a credit card responsibly as a resource for convenience when dealing with emergencies or making quality purchases that I needed to bring value to my life. No matter what, always make the minimum payment before the due date, because these payments decrease the balance, however small. Now, your credit card statement shows you how long it will take to pay off the balance if you make just the minimum payment and if you make higher payments. Paying at least the minimum payment on time each month will help you to have a good credit score.

A credit card is a valuable resource that should be used to acquire experiences and purchase items that bring you personal value. When using a credit card, try to use only a portion of the credit limit; this will always look good to future creditors. Credit cards shouldn't be used as spending money on every day items like lunch or Friday night pizza. A credit card is a revolving loan. Meaning, once you pay on the balance you can use the card again. Unless, you are able to pay the full balance at the end of the month, you will pay interest on this loan. Since, you have to pay this loan back; you should be paying money back for something specific that added value to your life. The interest you pay on a credit card is the price of the convenience of using the card. However, you should not pay more interest than is necessary, so whenever possible pay more than the minimum amount due.

Credit cards allow for the satisfaction of an immediate desire. But, the main reason to have a credit card is to establish and maintain a positive credit history.

Establishing Credit

Credit is when you can obtain something of value now by borrowing money from a financial institution with the promise to make payments to that institution later. A credit card is an excellent account to establish a positive credit history. Credit cards are useful tools in your financial life and when used responsibly, can provide a pathway to attain the items or experiences you want without going beyond your ability to pay the credit card balance. There are many advantages to having a credit card, besides just making purchases. You may want to rent a car, reserve a hotel room or make online purchases with fraud protection. If you don't qualify for a traditional credit card, there are other options.

Unless, you are a college student and apply for a credit card while you are on campus, you have to find a way to establish credit. How do you establish credit when you are just getting started on your financial journey or you are rebuilding your credit, when life has taken an unexpected turn? There are two popular options most people have to establish credit without getting a traditional credit card. The first is to open a secured credit card and the second is to become an authorized user on an existing credit card account.

Secured Credit Cards

To obtain a secured credit card you are required to make a cash deposit in an interest bearing account with a credit card company in the amount of your desired credit limit. This deposit gives lenders confidence that you will pay the monthly credit card bill. This refundable deposit is collateral for your credit limit. For example, if you want a credit limit of $300, you are required to make a deposit of $300. This financial product will allow you to build credit by using the credit card and making on time payments. After you build a history with the card, you can request that your credit card be converted to an unsecured credit card and your deposit will be refunded. By making on time minimum payments and staying under the credit limit, you are making positive steps towards a good credit history.

The credit card company will report your good account activity to the three major credit bureaus; Transunion, Experian and Equifax. This activity will be displayed on your credit report, showing all future creditors that you are capable of handling the responsibility of credit. A secured credit card will also help you with developing good credit habits. Keep in mind that each credit card company has different lending standards for their secured cards. Some companies that offer secured credit cards are Capital One and Discover.

Authorized User

The other option available to people trying to establish credit is to become an authorized user. If you have a parent or spouse that has a good credit history with a credit card account you can ask them to become an authorized user. This method allows you to benefit from their good credit record. The cardholder simply calls the credit card company and makes a request for your name to be added to the account.

You can receive a credit card in your name and as long as you pay for the purchases you make, your parent or spouse should be comfortable with adding you to the account. All of the activity from the credit card will be recorded on your credit report and this activity will also be incorporated into your credit score.

When a person is added to the account they are not legally responsible for the additional charges made on the account. It is important to be mindful not to overspend as an authorized user. The primary cardholder is still responsible for the payments. As long as the primary cardholder continues to make the payments on time and keeps the credit balance below 33% of the credit limit, this positive activity will be reported to the credit reporting agencies. For example, if the credit limit is $1,500, the balance should not be more than $500 for longer then the grace period to the next billing cycle.

Pursuing this option will result in a positive credit score for everyone on the account. The opposite is also true, if the primary cardholder doesn't maintain a good payment record, it will negatively affect the authorized user's credit history.

The primary cardholder must be assured that you are responsible and won't try to spend all the credit on the card. Remember, the primary cardholder is the only person legally responsible for all purchases made on the account. Again, they have the option on whether or not to give you a card. Either way, you will still benefit from the credit history and activity when you are an authorized user.

Both secured credit cards and becoming an authorized user are excellent options to establishing or reestablishing credit. Credit card accounts have one of the biggest impacts on your credit score. Both of these methods will improve your credit report and credit score.

Credit Reports

A credit report is a summary of your financial record and payment history at any given point in time. Much like a photograph, it is a snap shot of your credit history. Potential lenders will use your credit report to help them evaluate whether or not you are a good credit risk to lend money. Creditors will also determine the terms of the loan, such as the interest rate and the length of the loan based on what is on your credit report.

The three major credit bureaus are Experian, Equifax, and Transunion. These agencies collect certain types of information about you, beginning with your personal information, name, address, social security number and your place of employment. Your use of credit and information from the public record are primarily the information that is included on your credit report. Other information on your credit report will also include; how often you make on time payments, the total amount of credit you have, how much credit you have available and whether a debt or bill collector is collecting money from you. It will also contain information on any liens, judgments or bankruptcies you may have, which provides insight into your financial obligations.

Most credit reports are divided into five sections. These sections include the following:

1. **Identifying information.** This includes your name and current and past addresses, social security number, date of birth and some job history, but not all of your employment history will appear. It will not include race, martial status, ethnicity, religion or sexual orientation.

2. **Public record information.** This section includes public record data of financial importance, including consumer bankruptcies, judgments and state and federal tax liens. Other public records that usually do not appear on credit reports are marriage records, adoptions, and records of civil suits that have not resulted in judgments.

3. **Collection agency accounts information**. This section will show if you have or have had any accounts with a collection agency and the status of those accounts.

4. **Credit account information.** This section will include accounts you have now or that you had before with creditors of credit cards and installment loans. Credit cards are revolving loans and installment loans are loans that have a set payment schedule such as car loans, mortgages and student loans. The accounts listed will include the following:

> The company name, account number, date opened, last activity, type of account and status, date closed if the account is no longer open, the credit limit, any amount currently owed and whether you are current

or late on payments, how many times you have made late payments (either 30, 60 or 90 days) and the most recent balance.

It is important to make sure what is listed is your information and that it is correct. There are procedures to follow if the information is in anyway incorrect, which will be discussed in detail later.

5. Inquiries made to your account. When you apply for credit and a lender reviews your credit report, it is listed as an "inquiry" on your report. When you request a copy of your own report it is not listed as an inquiry and doesn't count against you with your credit score. You will also see promotional inquires and periodic reviews of your credit history by one or more of your creditors, these are also not official inquiries.

The following are the mailing addresses, phone numbers and websites of the three main credit reporting agencies.

Equifax Information Services
P.O. Box 740256
Atlanta, GA 30348
(866) 349-5191
www.equifax.com

Experian
P.O. Box 4500
Allen, TX 75013
(888) 397-3742
www.experian.com

Trans Union
P.O. Box 2000
Chester, PA 19016
(800) 680-7289
www.transunion.com

You can request your credit report anytime, from any one of these three agencies. It is a good idea to check all three reports, because the information may differ on each report. There is a small fee each agency charges for a copy of your report. You should check your credit reports at least once a year.

There is only one website that will issue you a free copy of all three credit reports once a year; it is **www.annualcreditreport.com**. On the website you can also download a form, print, complete and mail it to receive your credit reports in the mail. You can also call to ask for your credit report at **(877) 322-8228**.

Mail the completed form to:
Annual Credit Report Request Service
P.O. Box 105281
Atlanta, GA 30348

Credit Scores

Credit scores sum up the information on your credit report into a three-digit number. The score is the result of a complex mathematical formula. Credit scores are used as an additional tool along with your credit report for creditors to evaluate your credit worthiness. FICO scores, which are calculated using a formula, owned by Fair Isaac Corporation, are the most commonly used credit scores. These scores range from 350 to 850. A FICO score above 650 is considered a decent score by most creditors and 750 or above is the best score.

The following chart, illustrates how your credit report is used to calculate your score:

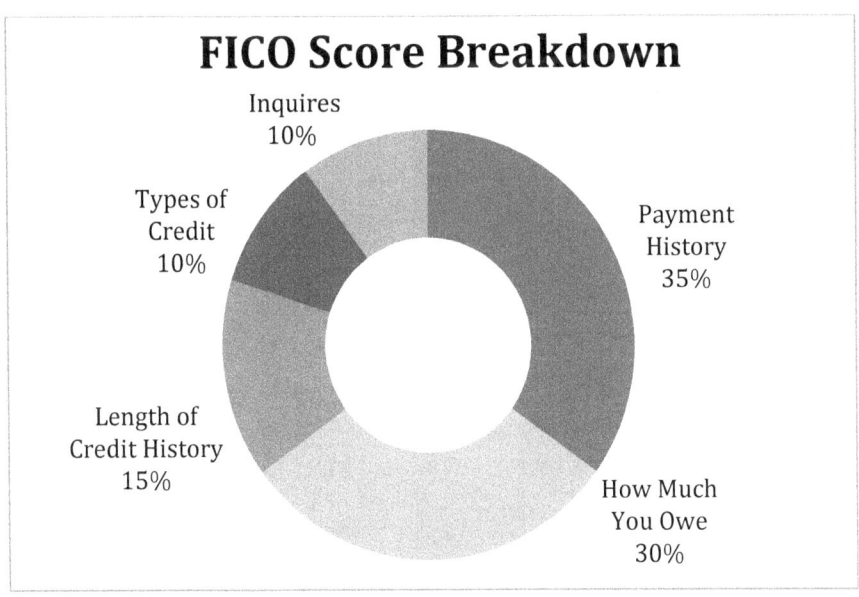

Payment History (35%)
Payment history is the largest factor in calculating your credit score; it evaluates whether you pay your bill on time and as agreed. The impact on your score from a single late or missed payment decreases over time. Paying your bills on time will help increase your score.

How Much Money you Owe (30%)
The next biggest factor in calculating your credit score is the total amount you owe on loans and credit cards. This includes the amount

you are paying down on loan balances as agreed. It also includes your credit utilization rate. Your credit utilization rate is how much of your available credit you are using. Maintaining a 33% utilization rate of your credit cards and maintaining the payment schedule on your installment loans, will contribute to a healthy credit score.

Length of Credit History (15%)

The next factor that impacts your score is the length of good standing credit accounts. Your score increases the longer your credit history is. The more established credit accounts you have in good standing the better the impact on your score. Remember, keep old accounts in good standing open; this will help your credit score.

Types of Credit (10%)

Your FICO score increases if you have both credit cards (revolving credit) and loans (installment loans, such as a mortgage, student loans or car loan) in good standing. Generally, it is considered a positive to have a mortgage, an auto loan, and no more than six credit cards.

Inquires (10%)

When you apply for credit, you are giving permission to a creditor to view your credit report. This request is listed on your credit report as an inquiry. This action has a small effect on your credit score. These types of inquiries stay on your credit report for two years. As previously stated, creditors look at your credit report when they offer you a special promotional rate or credit increase. When you request a copy of your own report, these are not recorded as an "inquiry" and don't count against your credit score.

Credit reports and the FICO credit score are critical functions of your financial life. They control whether you get approved for credit at a low interest rate, high interest rate or approved at all.

Both must be maintained and taken seriously on your financial journey. If your credit situation ever gets out of control, there are steps you can take to get back on track.

Credit Repair

Repairing your credit can be an overwhelming proposition. If you follow a few rules you will be able to fix your credit without spending hundreds of dollars with a company. There are no quick fixes when it comes to repairing your credit. A company that promises to erase any thing off your credit that is your account is not being completely honest with you. The only way to repair your credit is with time, effort and sticking to a personal debt repayment plan. You didn't get into trouble with your credit overnight and you can't get out of it overnight. Remember, the debt you have is a result of decisions that were a good idea, or not, at one time. Paying the money back is as simple as developing a plan and sticking to it. Whether you seek help from a company or do it yourself, it will require a plan.

The following are primary steps to take to improve your credit report and scores.

1. Request a free copy of your credit report from the three credit reporting agencies at **www.annualcreditreport.com**

2. Use the credit repair letters at the end of this book to dispute

any incorrect information on your credit report.

3. Pay the amount due before the due date on all your loans and credit cards; this represents 35% of your credit score.

4. Stop using your credit cards. Get your credit card balances under their limits, even if the credit utilization is not under 33%. Paying down the balance even to 50% will improve your credit score.

5. Stop applying for new credit. No new inquiries for the time you are improving your credit.

6. Finally, keep all paid off good standing accounts open. Paid off bad debt stays on your credit report for 7 years.

Steps 3 and 4 represent 65% of your credit score. Your credit score can be improved with your own efforts. You can do the work it takes to have the credit score you want. The money spent on a credit repair company could be used to pay down your debt.

Credit was invented for you to make the purchases you want beyond the cash you have at the moment. Credit is the bridge to what you want now, but are willing to pay a little more for later. The key is to balance the payments with the rest of the things you have to spend your money on to live. If you didn't buy things with credit, would you make these same purchases in cash or would you make them at all? Credit is a resource that should be respected for the difference it makes in your life.

4

The Loans

"Happiness is where we find it, but very rarely where we seek it."
~J. Petit Senn

The sun was shining upon my face driving down Route 70 in New Jersey, I was happy as could be. I had recently married the best woman I have ever known. We had just returned from our honeymoon to a Caribbean island. Suddenly, the car started making a noise coming from under the hood. We made it home only to discover the exhaust pipe was loose. We took the car to the local dealership. Fortunately, the car was still under the manufacturers warranty. The service department was able to repair the car that day. However, the repairs didn't seem to work and the problem continued. After a few more visits with no ability to fix the car, we decided it was time for another car. Now, this would be our first major purchase as a married couple, so the pressure was on for it to be a good decision. Whatever the decision we both agreed it had to be unanimous. Before visiting the dealership we agreed on how much we wanted to spend and the payment we were comfortable with. Armed with this information, the next Saturday we went to a dealership. Upon entering the dealership we were greeted by an older gentleman with a full head of grey hair. After he showed us a few new cars and we test drove a few used cars, our choices for our next vehicle came down to a 2004 Toyota Camry or a 2006 Lexus

ES350 sedan with the gold trim package. Both vehicles were very close in price, however it was 2008; the mileage on the two vehicles was the main difference to consider. The Toyota had 34,000 miles and the Lexus had 62,000 miles. On average a car shouldn't have more than 14,000 miles driven per year. Also, the Toyota was under a manufacturers warranty and the Lexus was not. So, clearly the Toyota was the best choice. The salesman gave us a few minutes to discuss this pivotal decision.

My first thought was that we were making a decision not between two different vehicles, but the competing ideas of projecting an image of success and luxury versus practical and sensible. I was confronted by all of my past ideas of what I thought "making it" looked like. It certainly looked more like a Lexus than a Toyota. My desire to attain an automotive symbol of luxury haunted me like the ghosts of past dreams of riding in style and of forgotten rides on public transportation. In those few seconds, I had to think about the first major purchase of my new marriage and make a good decision. A decision based on my future with my new wife and not based on my ideas and baggage of the past. In the end we chose the Toyota. The practical choice won the day.

The salesman ran our credit and we were able to get the payment we wanted and with a good interest rate. They gave us $200 for our trade-in. That was a little bit of a shock, because I knew the tires alone were worth more than $200. Nevertheless, we were both very excited about our new vehicle. That day, I was reminded that financial decisions are a mixture of facts, expectations and emotions. The deal and the numbers all have to add up to make a good decision.

Loans

In your lifetime you will apply for many loans. Whether those loans are revolving or installment, they are chosen based on your needs and emotions, like choosing between a Lexus and a Toyota. Mortgages, auto loans, and student loans are all used to improve your life with shelter, transportation and education. It is important to make wise choices that provide you with the balance between the payments and the rest of your financial life.

These loans all have a set payment and a set interest rate. The lower the interest rate the lower the overall cost of the loan. As previously stated, your credit score will determine the terms of these loans. The higher your score the better the terms of the loan.

Buying a Car

Buying a car is a major purchase. Many factors are considered when making this purchase. The price of the vehicle and the monthly payments are just the beginning factors you should consider. Annual registration, gasoline costs, insurance and repairs not covered by the manufacturers warranty should also be factored into your decision when purchasing an automobile. You should start by using websites like Kelley Blue Book, **www.kb.com** or Edmunds, **www.edmunds.com** to do the research on the vehicles you are interested in purchasing. Having this information to negotiate a good deal on the purchase price, the features and options available on the vehicle is the most important start to the process. Unlike a used car a new car loses value the first day you drive it off the dealers lot. That is why you have to be comfortable with the price based on how long you plan to own the vehicle and factoring in the future trade in value. Remember, the purchase price is just as important as the payment and the interest rate on the loan. You should get a good deal on all the terms of the transaction.

Now that you have determined which car you are going to buy, you are comfortable with the car's price and you have a good idea how much you want to pay each month, here are some steps you want to consider before going to the dealership.

1. Request a copy of your credit report and credit score from any of the three credit reporting agencies. These reports will give you an excellent idea of what your interest rate may be based on your credit score.

2. Check the current auto loan interest rates at several banks, credit unions or other lenders. You can also look online at sites like **www.bankrate.com**, which may give you an estimate of interest rates nationwide and by your zip code.

3. Consider a down payment. Making a down payment will reduce the total amount you will finance, because you will be required to borrow less money.

4. Decide if you want to trade in your current vehicle. If you already own a vehicle, research its value to see how much you might get from a trade-in or private sale. If you owe more on your current auto loan than the car is worth you may want to reconsider a new purchase until your current loan is paid off.

Auto Loan Financing

You are now ready to pursue buying your next vehicle. While some people are able to pay cash for their new vehicle, most people will use financing. Understanding the loan process and knowing your options will assist you in saving money. You can shop around for financing even before you shop for a vehicle.

For example, bringing a couple of different loan quotes or pre-approvals from your bank or credit union to the dealer will place you in a stronger bargaining position to negotiate favorable financial terms with the dealer. With these options you can choose to stick with the offer you brought in or accept the dealers financing.

Deciding which option to choose may be confusing, because with a new car, manufacturers and dealers offer a wide variety of promotional finance deals. Consider any special deal as a starting point, especially when there's a choice between cut-rate financing and a manufacture's rebate. Always ask to have the fine print explained on a special deal. Here are some questions you should ask about the auto financing being offered.

1. What's the interest rate I'm paying over the life of the loan? The interest rate is also known as the annual percentage rate (APR).

2. Are there penalties with the loan? Is paying off the loan early considered a penalty?

3. What is the precise price I'm paying for the vehicle?

4. What is the total amount being financed? Taking into account your trade in, down payment and dealer's rebates.

5. What is the exact amount of each payment?

6. What is the total number of payments, how many years is the loan?

7. Does this loan offer "Gap Insurance"? In case of an accident and the car is totaled, gap insurance pays you the difference between what your insurance company gives you and the remaining balance on your loan.

Purchasing an automobile either new or used is a major commitment both financially and emotionally. We all want the best deal and the nicest choice. These steps are a good guideline for when you are in the market to make this very important decision. If purchasing a car is not an option you want to exercise, there is another path to having a vehicle in your life, which is to lease it.

Leasing a Car

Leasing a car is having the ability to drive a car without owning it. Leasing also allows you to have a newer or more luxurious automobile than you would have if you purchased it. If your desired car payment is $350 a month your choice may be in the Honda and Toyota range both new and used. However, leasing at this price point may have your choices expanded to Acura, Lexus and the entry models of Mercedes and BMW. With the leasing option you have the opportunity to take advantage of that new American tradition of

"Affordable Luxury". A phrase born in America for everyone to drive a vehicle that they would otherwise not purchase either because of the cost of the monthly payment or the maintenance and gas cost or both.

If you are going to lease your next vehicle there are a few factors to weigh before signing the paperwork. Keep in mind the following rules and you should have an enjoyable leasing experience.

1. One of the main factors about leasing a car to consider is the total miles you drive per year. Typically, the leasing contract will only allow 10,000 miles to 12,000 miles, with a charge per every mile after that in the range of 10 cents to 30 cents. If your commute is a good distance or you visit relatives in far away places often, these things have to be factored into your decision.

2. The term of your lease should not exceed the term of the bumper-to-bumper warranty, which is usually 3 years. Limit the lease to 24 to 36 months.

3. You are expected to return the vehicle in good shape when the lease expires. If there is more damage than just normal wear and tear you will be charged for the repairs. It is important to return the car in excellent condition.

4. Always remember to buy gap insurance on a leased car.

In many cases leasing a car gives you the opportunity to drive a luxury vehicle. Having a luxury car in America is one of the most desired and emotional purchases most people will ever make.

Leasing allows for a lower monthly payment, no matter what kind of car it is. And it gives you an opportunity for you to stay within your budget. It also allows you to have a new car more often, without worrying about maintenance over the long term.

Growing up, my father worked as a Correctional Officer in the Philadelphia prisons. He made a good wage and it provided him with a good benefit plan. One day, he decided he didn't want to own an ordinary automobile any longer. Armed with his federal income tax refund check, he proceeded to trade in his white 1982 Buick Skylark. Instead, he decided to purchase the most luxurious and extravagant automobile produced in 1984; a royal blue with blue interior Lincoln Town Car. At this time the only large luxury automobiles on the road were Mercedes, BMW and Cadillac, but in 1984 the Lincoln Town Car was king. Now this car was more than just transportation, it was a status symbol of the highest degree. Riding in this car was like floating down the street in a living room with seats softer than a cloud. Everywhere we went he was no longer Sam London the Correctional Officer; but he was often referred to by his nickname "Smash". "Smash with the Lincoln", became a part of his identity. "I deserve this car", he would exclaim. It was the first time I would witness someone being treated differently because of a possession. Those were some good times cruising around Philadelphia with my dad visiting family and enjoying the day.

One day, in what felt like a flash, the car was gone. At the end of the loan, he decided to trade the Lincoln in for another Buick, this time paying cash. He realized that there were better uses for his money than paying a car payment. When he no longer had the car, I don't know who was sadder; him or me. That experience taught me that there is a constant struggle to maintain a balance with every major purchase in your life. My dad made a decision to own a car based solely on emotion and how it made him feel. He wanted to own an item, but not just any item, a Lincoln Town Car that justified the hard work he did every day and made him feel good about living life.

We all want to make good decisions with money; the practical decision is always the hardest choice to accept. Any decision based purely on how it makes you feel, has to be based in the reality of your financial picture, so you can continue to feel good about the decision.

When working towards a goal, whether it is a luxury car or a quality education, loans help make these things possible. You should always be in search of the balance to maintain the payments with your emotional choices.

Student Loans

Going to college is part of the American dream. Acquiring some form of education is the only way to the good life in America. Whether it is a college education or a training program. My grandmother Pauline used to say to me all the time, "Learn how to do something for a living and do it well". Choosing a school to attend after high school is a decision made up of many factors. How far is the school? Do they have my major? And, of course how much is the tuition, room and board? Obtaining education after high school has become very expensive in the 21st century. Finding a way to pay for this very necessary next step in your life is a challenge.

What are Student Loans?

The cost of higher education has increased over the years. It may be very expensive to attend the school of your choice. There are many options for funding your education including; cash, grants, scholarships and student loans. Student loans are available for paying tuition and other fees at a college, university or school of higher education.

Student loans are a part of a student's financial aid package to help fund their education. For most federal student loans you have a six month grace period before you have to start making payments on your loans after you complete or stop going to school. There are many kinds of student loans to choose from such as Direct Subsidized, Direct Unsubsidized and PLUS Loans to name a few.

Types of Student Loans

The Stafford Loan program is the largest and most popular loan program available to students. There are two types of Stafford loans; subsidized and unsubsidized. Subsidized means the federal government pays the interest while the student is in school, for up to six months after graduation, and if necessary for a period of deferment. Subsidized loans are awarded based on financial need as determined by the Free Application for Federal Student Aid (FAFSA) form. The interest on this loan will vary between 3% and 6%. Unsubsidized loans mean students are responsible for interest payments from the start of signing for the loan. While pursuing a degree or certificate program a student can allow the interest to roll into the principal. For more information on these student loans, visit

www.studentaid.ed.gov. Parents have a federal loan option to help with the cost of college for their children, which is the Parent Loans for Undergraduate Students (PLUS).

Private lenders also issue student loans. The popular lenders are Sallie Mae, Wells Fargo and Bank of America. With private lenders the interest rate may be higher than the federal student loans.

Loan Repayment Options

Once upon a time there was only one option available to a borrower to repay their student loans; a set interest rate and a set payment schedule for ten years. But now there are five popular options to choose from, which are the following:

1. **Standard repayment plan**. Most borrowers start with this payment plan. This repayment plan has fixed payments and a set time frame to repay.

2. **Graduated repayment plan.** The payment begins at a lower amount for the first year and gradually increases every two years for up to 10 years.

3. **Extended repayment plan**. The payment is fixed or graduated for up to 25 years. The monthly payments are lower than the standard or graduated repayment plans, however, you will pay more interest over the life of the loan.

4. **Income-Based Repayment plan (IBR)**. The payment is based on your annual income, as your income decreases and

increases, so does your payment. After 25 years of consistent payments, the loan will be forgiven.

5. **Consolidation loan**. With this option you pay off of your existing federal student loans with a new loan. This simplifies the paperwork and payment you have to keep up with by reducing your payments to one payment. These loans can go up to 30 years.

Forbearance and Deferments

There may be times when you are unable to pay your student loan. You may be eligible for a deferment or forbearance of your payments. With a deferment, your lender grants you a temporary suspension of your payments for a specific reason such as unemployment, temporary disability, military service or a return to graduate school on a full-time basis. A deferment could last up to six months. With forbearance, your lender grants you permission to reduce or stop your loan payments for a certain time at their discretion, usually for an economic hardship.

From auto loans to student loans all of these payments are decisions to give your money to things in your life that provide improvement though education and transportation. They have to fit comfortably into your financial plan. Think carefully and cautiously about these long-term debt obligations. They both impact your credit report and credit score as installment loans.

5

The Home

"The most difficult thing is the decision to act the rest is merely tenacity."

~Amelia Earhart

When I met the woman who would become my wife, I lived in an apartment just outside Philadelphia in a quiet suburb and she owned a house in New Jersey. After we were married, I moved in with her because her house was much bigger than my apartment. I really liked that house, it was in a quiet neighborhood and it was big enough to blend our belongings and furniture. However, I always knew we would buy our own home together. About a year into being married we realized that the house was indeed too small for our growing life together. The time had come, sooner than I thought, that we were going to start looking for our home to purchase together. But, where would we live? How much would we spend? And what about acquiring a mortgage? The thought of buying our home was both exciting and scary at the same time.

There were many things to think about; first we had to decide where we wanted to live. Well, I never imagined buying a house anywhere else but Philadelphia, Pennsylvania, but with marriage comes compromise. I had to consider and listen to what my wife thought. We both agreed the decision on the house had to be unanimous. Like the automobile purchase we both had to agree. This was going to be the most important financial decision of our marriage and our lives.

After looking at house listings online, we started driving through different neighborhoods in Philadelphia and Southern New Jersey. It was the fall of 2008, a few weeks after the U.S. stock market lost 700 points in one day and the financial crisis was about to effect the entire economy. But, we had a house to sell and another one to buy; circumstances we couldn't control wouldn't discourage us.

One day, we went to an open house in Southern New Jersey. The listing agent asked if we had a real estate agent to help with our search. We later hired her to sell our house, while we continued to look for our new home. At this time we had settled on looking at houses in a Philadelphia up and coming neighborhood and in Southern New Jersey. Even though we should have done this first, we went to figure out how much house we could afford. The rule of thumb, our real estate agent told us, was "Your mortgage will usually be about 1% of the purchase price of the house". We used the online calculator at **www.bankrate.com** to add in the taxes and insurance to figure out a mortgage payment that we were comfortable with. With that information in hand, we were able to narrow our search down to a few neighborhoods.

After the house was on the market for over seven months and a few offers fell through, we were starting to get discouraged. One day, our agent called to tell us we received an offer from a newlywed couple and with the blink of any eye our house was sold. We didn't have a house to buy and in 45 days we wouldn't have a place to live. The closing date was set in stone because the buyer had to leave their apartment. To say panic was setting in was an understatement. We were constantly looking for possible houses to buy and trying to make a good decision for our family.

We finally agreed that we could get more for our money in New Jersey than anything we had seen in Philadelphia. I didn't have time to dwell on the realization that my first home I was purchasing was not going to be in Philadelphia. A few days later we made an offer on a house in Southern New Jersey and after a few counteroffers with the seller's agent our offer was rejected. All because they were unwilling to give us seller assist at closing, they let the deal go for a few thousand dollars. Back to square one. Now, we are only 21 days away from selling our home. We were coming down to the wire.

Our agent sent us listings everyday and we told her about houses we wanted to see. One evening after work we went to see two houses in one of the towns in Southern New Jersey. The first house was a disappointment; the pictures online were very misleading. The second house had potential and was in a good location. It met all our requirements including the advice we received from my mother-in-law, "Make sure the school district is good, that will determine whether the value of your house keeps rising". We made an offer on the house and a few days later it was accepted with a seller assist. The only problem now, was figuring out when we would close on the house we wanted to buy, because we were scheduled to close on the house we were selling in 17 days. We needed a miracle.

Well, the buyers of our house were coming from an apartment and the seller's of the new house were going to an apartment out of state. Our agent was selling our home and representing us with buying our new home. The real estate agency's mortgage company was financing the mortgage and we were able to close on both houses on the same day!

The closing date came and we were very excited. We were in the first closing for two hours signing what seemed like an endless sea of paper. It felt good to get the check from the proceeds of selling the house; even though we had to turn over that check in a few hours to buy the new house. In the time between the first and second closing it occurred to me that in the last 15 months we had gotten married, bought a car and now we were about to buy a house in suburban New Jersey. I felt overwhelmed, excited and nervous all at the same time. This had been a world wind experience with the very real feeling of moving further into adulthood upon me, there was no turning back.

The second closing went well. We were now homeowners once again! We drove to our home and unpacked the U-Haul truck. The next morning I went outside to look around and soak in my new surroundings. As I looked around, it suddenly occurred to me, who is going to cut all this grass?

Deciding to Buy a House

Owning a home is a very personal decision filled with both past and present emotional thoughts. The choice between owning and renting is a never-ending narrative of pros and cons. However, the two main factors in this decision are qualifying for a mortgage and deciding if the upkeep and maintenance of a home is for you. Home ownership has many privileges, whether or not it is for you, is up to you. However, it should be considered at some point in your lifetime. The decision to purchase a home is the most serious and expensive transaction most people will ever make. You are giving your money to a mortgage for 30 years, if you complete the average length of a loan. The mortgage payment is only one of many factors to consider. Property taxes, maintenance and buying furniture also have to be considered when buying a home.

What is a Mortgage?

There are many factors and issues with buying a house. But, your ability to pay the mortgage every month and on time is the most important factor, because without that, the rest is unimportant. A mortgage is a loan that a bank or credit union issues you to purchase a house, while using the home as collateral for the loan. The mortgage payment includes; principle, interest, homeowners insurance and mortgage insurance (if you make a down payment of less than 20%). The most traditional and safest mortgage is a 30 year fixed rate mortgage. This mortgage payment will stay the same throughout the life of the loan. A fixed rate mortgage is very straightforward and easy to understand. All other types of mortgages are either riskier or the payment will be higher. The stability of the fixed payment schedule will allow you to properly budget for other expenses.

How Much Mortgage do I Need?

Once you have decided that buying a house is the next financial move you want to make, the first three things you need are patience, thoughtful planning and good decision-making. You will need all three on your journey to homeownership.

The next step to homeownership is figuring out how much house you can afford; even before you check your credit. Why is this? Your ability to pay the mortgage is the most important factor. Using an online calculator at **www.bankrate.com** enter your current rent as a starting point for your monthly payment and using an interest rate you find online, you will be able to determine how much house you can afford. This will give you a good idea of how much mortgage you are comfortable with paying each month.

For example, if your current rent is $750 a month, you can use that amount to determine your mortgage amount. With an interest rate of 4% over 30 years, your mortgage loan amount will be around the $150,000 range. With a down payment of 3.5% ($5,250), the homeowners insurance and the property taxes, the total payment will be about $750 in most parts of the United States. This payment will be reasonable for your house purchase because you currently make this in rent payments. With this payment, you are still able to maintain your current budget. The calculator from Bankrate will give you a price point to aim towards and it will let you know your comfort range for the price of your house. Now, let's discuss the next important step, the home buying process.

The Home Buying Process

Checking your credit report and credit score with all three credit agencies before you call a lender is the next task on your checklist. The higher the score the better the interest rate is going to be. Generally, you need at least a 640 FICO score for a decent interest rate on a mortgage loan. There are loans available for lower FICO scores, however the interest and fees on those loans will be higher.

The Real Estate Agent

Since you have checked your credit and you have an idea of the mortgage payment you are comfortable with, it is time to find a real estate agent in the area you are interested in living. The agent should be very familiar with the surrounding area and know the temperature of the market, meaning they should know which houses are selling, how good the schools are and which houses are available in your price range in the area you are interested in. The agent is your partner in the search for your new home. They will be able to guide you through most of the home buying process.

You will meet with a lender to get pre-approved, which will allow you to know how much house you can afford based solely on your credit and financial well being. The lender will have you fill out a standard loan application.

Uniform Residential Loan Application

The Uniform Residential Loan Application is the standard loan application for applying for a mortgage. This is the application to receive your mortgage loan pre-approval from a lender. There are 10 sections to complete on the application.

1. **Type of Mortgage and Terms of the Loan**. The information in this section should match the type of mortgage loan and terms that you discussed with your loan officer.

2. **Property Information and Purpose of Loan.** This section is for when you select a property. You will provide the

address, the year the house was built, whether this is a purchase or a refinance and detail about the mortgage you want.

3. **Borrower Information**. This section is for the borrower to provide their social security number, date of birth, marital status, and contact information.

4. **Employment Information**. All borrowers need to provide two years of employment history.

5. **Monthly Income and Combined Housing Expense Information**. You will provide your pay stubs and your monthly bills that are reported on your credit report, along with your federal tax returns from the last two years. With this information, your loan officer will determine your ability to make regular payments on your mortgage including the other costs associated with owning a home.

6. **Asset and Liabilities.** This section indicates your current financial position. How much you own (assets) versus how much you owe (liabilities). The difference between the two is your net worth. Examples of assets include your savings account and 401(k) account and liabilities are bills that are on your credit report such as credit cards and student loans. Copies of the statements for all these accounts are required.

7. **Details of the Transaction.** This section provides the details of the mortgage. The loan officer will complete this information, which includes the purchase price of the house, closing costs, and the total cost of the mortgage.

8. **Declarations.** This includes any pending or past financial legal matters.

9. **Acknowledgment and Agreement**. All borrows sign the application stating they understand the terms.

10. **Information for Government Monitoring Purposes**. You will need to provide information such as your ethnic origin and race. Because the U.S. government has to, by law, make sure the housing finance system meets the needs of every racial and ethnic group in America.

The Pre-Approval

This application should result in the lender offering you a pre-approval for the amount of mortgage you qualify for. Once you have your pre-approval in writing you are able to continue looking at houses in the price range you are interested in, but now you can submit an offer. Keep in mind your pre-approval is good for between 45 and 60 days.

Make an Offer

Once you find the house you want, move quickly to make your offer. Work with your agent to devise the best strategy to make a fair offer you think the buyer will accept. Try not to go too low from the asking price, while still giving the seller room to negotiate, especially if are asking for assistance with the closing cost. Once the offer is accepted you are one step closer.

Enter the Contract

Your agent or lawyer will review this document to make sure the deal is contingent upon you obtaining a mortgage, a home inspection that shows no significant defects and a guarantee that you will conduct a walk-through inspection within 24 hours before the closing date. You also need a good faith deposit of 1% of the purchase price or $1,000, which will be deposited into an escrow account. This deposit is non-refundable except in cases where a particular item was not met.

Secure the Loan

Now you can call your mortgage lender and agree on the terms that were talked about during the pre-approval process. This is when you decide to choose a fixed rate mortgage and whether to pay points to lower the rate. Points are 1% of the mortgage fee that a lender may charge to lower the interest rate on the loan. Expect to pay $50 to $75 for a credit check and $150 to $300 for an appraisal of the house. Most other fees will be paid at the closing. This is also the point where you secure your homeowners insurance policy quote.

Get an Inspection

In addition to the appraisal that the mortgage lender is requesting, you should hire your own home inspector. An inspection costs about $300, on average, and takes at minimum two hours to complete. The home inspection will discover any minor to major repairs that are needed, but will not delay the purchase of the house. If major repairs are discovered during the home inspection and the owner is unwilling or unable to correct them you have the right to back out of the whole deal. The costs to make these repairs can be negotiated and paid by the seller at closing.

The Closing Process

The closing or settlement is where all the paperwork is signed and checks are exchanged. Your settlement charges are divided into two categories, adjusted origination charges and settlement services.

Adjusted origination charges are the sum of your lender's origination charges and any credits or charges (ex: points) for the specific interest rate on your mortgage loan. These charges are stated as a percentage of the face value of the loan and cannot be changed at settlement.

Settlement services include most of your settlement charges. Some common fees in this section are:

1. **Title services fee and title insurance**. The fee paid to a title company to search county records to make sure the title to the property you are buying is clear and free of any complication like pending debts or liens on the property.

2. **Government recording charges**. The fee required to register the property under your name.

3. **Homeowners insurance**. This charge is for the insurance you must buy for the property to provide protection

from a loss, such as fire and storm damage. In many cases homeowners choose to let the lender pay the insurance from an escrow account the lender sets up for you.

There may be other fees associated with your settlement, be sure to review these with your loan officer to have a complete understanding of their meaning. Make sure you understand what you're signing. It is important to read the documents carefully. Always ask questions when you don't understand something. Please note that, the closing paperwork and process may vary depending upon the state you live in.

After you sign what seems like a thousand pieces of paper, you will be a proud homeowner. This is quite an accomplishment. Purchasing a house is a big deal. Make sure you take the responsibility seriously. Homeownership is the cornerstone of building wealth for the average person in America. Along with retirement savings, it is the next essential step on your financial journey.

6

Preparing for the Day

"I've learned that people will forget what you said, people will forget what you did, but people will never forget how you made them feel."
~Maya Angelou

It started out as a regular day, as I ran down a dusty Mississippi road with the sun beaming down on my sweat drenched face. I was in formation with my fellow sailors at training school, where we were preparing to be Ship's Serviceman in the United States Navy. Suddenly, I noticed a person running down from the top of the hill towards where we had stopped to take a break. The person asked, "Are you Mkemo London?" I said, yes. The next words out of his mouth are the 6 words that every member of the military fears hearing, "the Chaplain wants to see you." I was too new to the military, having only completed three months, to realize what was happening. When I walked into the Chaplain's office, he said that I should call home. I knew the number to my house because it hadn't changed in 14 years. The phone rang only three times, but somehow it seemed like an eternity. My mother picked up and on the other end, her voice sounded as if all the joy in the world had ended. She said, "Your brother has been in an accident, you have to come tomorrow." I asked with a cracked voice "Is he ok"? She just simply said, "You have to come home." The next morning I was on the first flight out of Meridian, Mississippi. Upon arriving in Philadelphia, I was greeted by my father, as we drove from the airport his face said it all. I asked, "How bad is it?" He just looked at me and said, "He's in pretty bad shape." We arrived at the hospital and to my surprise a lot of our friends and family were there, including, the mother of my brother's child, Stacy. As I entered the hospital room, my mother and our pastor, Dr. Leonard greeted me and at that moment, I knew that my best friend, the person in the world that believed in me no matter what, was gone. It was as if all the air in the room was sucked out and I couldn't breathe for what seemed like an eternity. The pastor said a prayer to bless my brother and we all exited the room. I was in a state of shock; I barely noticed my mother and Stacy crying on each other's shoulder. It was like I was dreaming, but this was real. And to make matters even worse, we didn't have any life insurance for my brother, because he was only 22. We had to rely on the kind contributions from friends and family. The lesson I learned from that horrible tragedy was the importance of everyone having life insurance. Death is a certainty for everyone; you have to be prepared for when the time comes.

Insurance

Insurance is one those things you pay every month and hope you never have to use. But, you are glad it is there in your time of need. Unlike homeowners insurance, car insurance or health insurance, life insurance is one of those things you only use once. However, life insurance is more than just protecting a family from financial hardship at a time of unimaginable loss, it can also serve as an investment for your future. There are a lot of different insurance policies and companies to choose from. Let's discuss the options.

The three key terms you need to know about insurance in general are coverage, premium and deductible.

1. **Coverage**. The amount of money the policy will pay you for whatever you are insuring, whether it's life, home or car. With life insurance, the coverage might be $100,000, meaning that when you pass away your beneficiary will receive a check for that amount.

2. **Premium**. Represents the cost of the coverage or how much you have to pay each month for the insurance policy. Though the coverage might be $100,000, your premium is only a small fraction of the coverage.

3. **Deductible**. How much money you have to come up with to help cover the cost of an insurable event. For example, if you have a $250 deductible on your auto insurance and you have an accident causing $1,000 in damage to the car, you're responsible for the first $250; the insurance company covers the rest. A deductible is not a part of life insurance.

Car Insurance

You have probably seen one or two commercials for insurance companies promising to save you money on your insurance premiums. They are able to do this because if you have a higher deductible your insurance premium will be lower.

For example, if your deductible goes from $500 to $1,000 you might save $14 per month. But, you will be responsible for the first

$1,000 if you have an accident. You are saving money in the short run, but you have to weigh the pros and cons of your own financial situation. Now let's discuss one of the most important insurances you will need, life insurance.

Life Insurance

Life insurance serves the purpose of providing financial relief to your beneficiaries by paying them the face value of the policy. With certain types of policies you can accumulate cash through the years that you can draw on later in life for things like a college education, a down payment on a home or a cash infusion into your retirement account. Ultimately, there are only two types of life insurance, term and cash value or permanent. There is an argument for both options; term life is the cheapest option for people of all ages to get coverage. On the other hand cash value policies offer an investment option that helps you build wealth. Within each of these categories, there are many different types of life insurance to choose from so that the coverage is more of a custom fit to your specific needs. Both types have a significant list of pros and cons.

Term Life Insurance

Term life insurance is definitely one of the most basic life insurance policies you can purchase. This is because term life only offers a death benefit and no cash value builds up in the policy and for this reason it is very inexpensive. Term life is in place for a specific number of years. That term is usually between 10 and 30 years, though longer terms are available. You pick the insurance coverage you need, such as $100,000 and you pay a premium either monthly or quarterly. Your beneficiary will be paid the face value of the policy at the end of your life.

The most popular version of term life insurance is called a **level term** policy. With this policy your premiums never change. The best feature of term life insurance is that it is the cheapest type of life insurance, meaning you can afford more coverage for a relatively small premium. The policy will end when the term ends and if you are still alive you will have to buy more insurance at a higher rate, because you are older. Make sure you have a policy with an auto renewal and no medical exam, this way your coverage will continue when the original term has ended. The following is an example of the cost of a typical term life insurance policy for a healthy adult.

For example, a 30-year-old male who is a healthy non-smoker might pay about $11 per month for a 20 year $100,000 term life policy.

Cash Value

Cash value life insurance is different from term insurance, because it offers both a death benefit and cash value component. It is life insurance that builds savings that accumulates over time. Because of this feature the cash value premiums for a similar amount of term life insurance is often four to eight times higher. The coverage in the previous example would climb from $11 a month to close to $100 a month. The popular types of cash value life insurance are Whole life and Universal life.

Whole Life Insurance

A whole life insurance policy is a type of cash value insurance that provides a guaranteed death benefit and has fixed premiums. This life insurance policy is sometimes known as a permanent or straight life insurance. The biggest difference this policy has with term life is a portion of the premium pays for the insurance and the rest accumulates tax deferred in a cash value account earning a fixed rate of interest. You may be able to borrow against the cash value when it reaches a certain balance. One thing to remember about borrowing money from this policy is any balance on the loan will reduce the death benefit. If you cancel the policy, you will receive the cash value of the policy minus any fees and expenses. The best reason by far to own a whole life insurance is the accumulated cash value.

Life insurance is usually associated with replacing the income of a loved one or covering final expenses. However, whole life insurance if purchased early in life, provides coverage for expenses, lower premiums and cash value.

For example, if you purchased a $50,000 whole life insurance policy for an 11-year-old child the premium would be around $40 a month. This provides two advantages; the policy will accumulate cash value that could be borrowed for college or a home down payment after the child is an adult and the cash value has built up over time. The other advantage is the young person will start life with an insurance policy where the premiums won't increase over their lifetime and cash will continue to accumulate. It is a great deal to set up for your children. And the younger the child is the cheaper the premium. The premium for the same $50,000 insurance policy for a 5 year old is about $10 a month; imagine that, paying $10 a month for $50,000 of life insurance for the rest of your life. This kind of insurance is about much more than just covering final expenses. It is an investment in preparing for life.

Universal Life Insurance

Universal life insurance is a type of cash value insurance that offers flexible premiums and a flexible death benefit. Your tax deferred cash value account accumulates interest at the guaranteed rate similar to whole life. However, the interest rate may be higher if the overall market interest rates are higher than the guaranteed rate, which is the rate whole life insurance is based on. The biggest difference between universal and whole life is the flexible premiums that allow you to adjust how much you'll pay each year, by having the option to access some of the policy's cash value, although you will always have to pay the minimum premium amount. Depending on the policy's cash value, it may be possible to skip a premium payment or let the cash accumulate in value over time. Also, there is a feature that allows you to increase or decrease the death benefit. Similar to whole life you are able to borrow money from the policy tax-free. The loan is paid back with the monthly premium payments.

The flexibility a universal life policy provides is a key difference over whole life. As a result, universal life insurance premiums are lower during periods of high interest rates than whole life insurance premiums, often for the same amount of coverage.

Life insurance is a very important part of your financial life; it provides peace of mind in a time of need. The sooner you purchase it for yourself, spouse and your children the cheaper it will be. Whole life and universal life provide more than just a death benefit, they provide the cash value option, which is very valuable in an emergency, just as your SAFE fund provides similar security. Whether you choose term life, whole life or universal life, the comfort of having this coverage is priceless while life insurance protects your family, there are other insurances that protect your belongings such as renters and homeowners insurance.

Renters Insurance

Many renters have the impression that if there is ever an emergency situation such as a fire or a burglary, the landlord's homeowners insurance will cover their belongings. Unfortunately, their insurance will only cover the damage done to the rental property and not the tenant's personal property. You will need a separate insurance policy to cover your possessions. Renters insurance is insurance that covers all your belongings in an apartment or house.

Renters insurance is relativity inexpensive with the average premium cost around $18 a month. For that price the policy usually covers fire, explosion, smoke, theft and most other damage that can occur. However, if you think there could be a flood, you have to purchase separate flood insurance. Next, consider how you want your belongs covered; actual cash value (ACV) or replacement cost coverage. Actual cash value only covers what your items were worth at the time of the damage. Replacement cost coverage will give you the money to buy all new items.

To make sure you are compensated for any belongings you may lose in the event something happens, be sure to take inventory of all your possessions. List each item, its value, and serial numbers as well as take photographs and videotape of each room. Keep receipts and all important items in a fireproof box or safe.

Homeowners Insurance

When purchasing a house you will be required to purchase a homeowners insurance policy at settlement and it will be a part of your closing costs. The main factor to remember with this policy is you want to elect the replacement cost coverage similar to the renters insurance. Also, elect the maximum coverage for your state for both the house replacement and your belongings. Consult the insurance agent about the details of the policy and make sure you fully understand everything that is included.

The principle of giving your money to the things that bring value to your life with credit cards, auto loans, student loans, a mortgage and insurance are all the results of decisions you make to shape your lifestyle. We have reviewed the areas that everyone should be aware of and consider when making financial decisions. Your credit score and credit report determine if the terms on these accounts and policies are favorable. These loans and policies are essential to achieving the balance and quality of life you seek. The management of your credit history affects all your choices for transportation, shelter, education and insurance. Even if your choices in the past have lead to credit difficulty, you always have a chance to make tomorrow better by making better choices today.

LIVE

Principle #3
Live within your income.

7

A Home for your Money

"Whatever we believe about ourselves and our ability comes true for us."

~Susan L. Taylor

Where did the time go? Just over five years and I'm finally getting out of the United States Navy with an Honorable Discharge. It was a time in my life filled with good experiences traveling the world and lessons of personal growth. But it was finally time to return to Philadelphia. Shortly, after arriving back home, I started my first real full time job with benefits and a salary. I got an accounting job at an unarmed security company. One of the initial moves I made after receiving my first paycheck was to open a checking account with direct deposit at a major bank. I did this for two reasons; I thought it was time to be an adult with a proper banking relationship with checks and a debit card and walking around Philadelphia with all cash was not a good idea. When I was in the Navy, most of my time was spent overseas and I always used the currency of whatever country I was visiting. Even though I still had the savings account from my youth, getting a checking account was the next level of my financial responsibility. I chose to use a large commercial bank for my checking account. I didn't have a monthly fee, because I set up direct deposit of my full net paycheck into the account. This was the first time I had a debit card. All my time in the Navy I had an ATM card, just to get cash out of the ATM. With a debit card I could access the money in my account by using the card at stores and online just like a credit card.

One day, a chain of events happened to remind me that a bank is a business. On my lunch break I went to buy a sandwich and a drink from my favorite Philly restaurant on Market Street. I used my debit card, and later that day, I made a withdrawal from the ATM for $20. The balance of the receipt indicated I had more in my account than I thought, so I immediately withdrew another $20. What I hadn't realized was not only did my lunch bill not come out of the account yet, but also my rent and credit card payment hadn't been taken out either. To my surprise my account was overdrawn leaving a negative balance of -$123. I was shocked because I didn't understand why my account had a negative balance. Well, the bank teller, who was very nice, explained to me that the bank paid the rent, credit card and lunch bill but since there was not enough money to cover all the transactions, I had to pay an insufficient funds fee for each transaction in the amount of $35. I asked how much money I was short to cover the transactions. When she said, $18 dollars, I was mad all over again. Apparently, all the transactions came in at the same time and the bank paid my rent first and the others next, but since they paid them all, I incurred the insufficient funds fees, which explained the negative balance amount. Fortunately, I was getting paid in a few days and the balance would be paid. This was a painful lesson. So, from that experience I rarely trust the ATM balance or the online bank balance. I keep track of my spending and when my bills are coming out of the account with my own Excel spreadsheet. One more thing I learned from that experience was to withdraw cash from the ATM once a week and to include that on my spreadsheet. It is important to remember that banks are in business to make money and one way is through overdraft and monthly maintenance fees.

They are not looking out for your best interest, so you have to.

Checking Accounts

Checking accounts are at the heart of your financial life. All the money you use to meet your financial needs can be paid from a checking account, from paying bills to buying groceries. How is a checking account different from a savings account?

A checking account comes with checks, which used to be the only method to pay most of your bills. They also come with a debit card, which is a card that looks like a credit card and is used to make purchases. However, debit cards simply give you access to the money in your account. Part, if not all of your paycheck should be directly deposited into this account. From there you can transfer money into your ME fund and your SAFE fund. Checking accounts also allow you to use online bill pay and/or the ability to pay your bills on the websites of your creditors. There are no restrictions on how often you access your cash, which is ideal for everyday use. Make sure you know the spending limits on your debit card and the maximum amount of daily withdrawals you are allowed to make from an ATM.

Where to Open your Checking Account?

Traditional Banks

Using a traditional bank for your checking account has the same advantages as I discussed earlier regarding choosing a savings account. It will allow you the convenience to access your money with ease and the ability to have a face-to-face meeting with a manager if there is a problem. Also, the FDIC insures this account. At traditional banks, please be aware of the fees associated with the account such as overdraft and daily minimum balances. The initial deposit amount for this type of account is usually $100 or less.

Credit Unions

A credit union is one of the most popular choices for a checking account in recent years, because unlike a traditional bank there are very little fees associated with this account. It takes a little research to find out if you are eligible to join a credit union. Like the savings account, a disadvantage to most credit unions is they usually have fewer locations than traditional banks. Also, the NCUA insures this account. The initial deposit amount can be as low as $15.

Checking Account Fees

Checking accounts like most financial accounts have fees and charges. The key is to find accounts at banks or credit unions that have low fees and a large ATM network. Unless you qualify for student checking, are associated with a particular employer or you have direct deposit at a large commercial bank, you will have to pay a maintenance fee of at least $10 a month. In addition, an ATM fee per transaction of at least $3 from the bank and another transaction fee from the ATM you are using will be assessed. It is always a good idea to use the ATM of the bank where you have your account; this is called an in-network ATM.

Overdraft fees are what people dislike the most about checking accounts. This is a fee that is charged if a bill or debit charge is presented to your account for payment and there is not enough money in the account to pay the item. The fee has increased in recent years to between $25-$39 per transaction. Most banks will pay the item and charge you a fee. Some financial institutions will not pay the item and still charge you the fee. Overdraft protection is offered by some institutions to protect against these fees by taking money from your savings account or line of credit. There are also some miscellaneous fees with checking accounts like ordering checks and requesting copies of prior monthly statements.

The main fact to remember most about checking accounts is to always know your balance. Don't rely on the online or ATM balance because it may not represent all the activity in the account. It is the only way to avoid the overdraft fees.

Prepaid Debit Cards

In recent years prepaid debit cards have become popular as an alterative to a traditional checking account at a bank or credit union. With this card you can load cash on to it and use it to pay bills and purchase items you need to live. You can also have direct deposit of your paycheck to a prepaid card. There are many fees associated with this financial product. Often, the fees with these cards are more than the fees with a traditional checking account. One resource to compare checking accounts to prepaid cards is **www.findabetterbank.com**.

The appeal of prepaid debit cards for many people seems to be the ease you can obtain the cards. Most times you can purchase a card at your local convenience store, as opposed to sitting down at a bank or credit union and filling out paperwork.

Another reason these cards are having such popularity, is they do not charge overdraft fees, making them appealing to people who may be tired of paying these fees on their regular checking account. If you are going to choose this option for your primary account, the best company for a prepaid card is American Express. They have two options available, Bluebird by American Express and American Express Serve. Both have the lowest fees among all the prepaid card options on the market.

An advantage banks and credit unions have over prepaid debit cards is they give you the ability to talk to a person face-to-face when it comes to dealing with a problem with your money. Establishing a checking account is essential for the management of your finances, but you have to monitor your spending to avoid unnecessary overdraft fees.

8

The Money Plan

One day, I was sitting in my apartment, listening to the Kind of Blue album by Miles Davis reminiscing on days gone by. When I went to collect my mail, I opened a letter from my student loan informing me of my pending payment and that my deferment was over. I received my credit card bill that was close to the limit and a few utility bills, which were due soon. And I still had to go grocery shopping. I suddenly realized that I might be in need of a budget. Having just started working my first job out of the military, I had to figure out how I was going to manage my new life and the financial responsibility that came with it.

Up until this point, I never needed a budget. I was in college, then I joined the military and I was basically hanging out and having a good time in my 20s. Now, it was time to get serious about my financial life and get on track. The only problem was I hated the idea of being on a budget. A budget seemed confining and limiting. My uncle Woody suggested that I write down everything that I spent to see where the money went. I tried that and it worked for a while. But, I still needed an overall plan for all my bills, spending money and savings. What I needed was a simple way to track my bills and spending money without worrying about every penny. Over the course of a few months, I developed the money plan.

The money plan is simply an outline for your money. It is divided into six sections.

1. Your **income**.

2. Your **savings** plan.

3. The **rent or mortgage**.

4. The accounts that affect your **credit** such as credit cards, auto loans and student loans.

5. Next, the bills for your **fixed expenses** like electric, cell phone and your insurances.

6. Finally, there is the **spending money** for the rest of life's expenses that vary from month to month, like groceries, transportation and other purchases.

Income

Calculating your monthly income from your employment is the first step to managing your money. If you are paid hourly, calculate the average amount of your check and multiply that by the number of weeks you are paid per month. Keep in mind if you are paid bi-weekly, twice a year, you are paid three times in a month and if you are paid weekly, four times a year, you are paid five weeks in a month. Payroll taxes such as social security, federal, state and local taxes along with medical and 401(k) deductions are taken from your gross income and the amount remaining is your net income. Everything in your money plan is based on your net income.

Savings

The first place your money should be deposited is to your ME fund and the SAFE fund automatically through direct deposit. Both accounts are set up at separate financial institutions from your main checking account. Remember, the amounts going to these accounts do not have to be large. You just have to put some money in each fund for both emergencies and your own personal use.

The House Payment

The rent or mortgage is a priority in your budget. Generally, this payment should not equal more than 30% of your net income. For example, if your monthly net income is $2,400 a month, your rent or mortgage should not be more than $720 per month.

One very important tip to remember is, do not attempt to pay your rent/mortgage out of one paycheck, commonly known as the "rent check". The key to money management is cash flow. Cash flow is when you manage your money in a way that has your bills paid on time and leaves you with enough money to function from day to day. You should split the payment of your rent/mortgage evenly with all the checks you receive in a month. For example, if your rent/mortgage is $700 a month and you get paid every two weeks set aside $350 from each check of the previous month, so you can pay your rent/mortgage on the 1st of the next month. For instance, when you set aside the $350 per check in March, you are now in position to pay your April rent/mortgage when it is due. This enables you to have peace of mind that your rent/mortgage is paid and you have money throughout the month giving you more room to maneuver.

Credit Expenses

These are all your fixed payments from your loans and credit cards. Student loans, car loans and credit cards are all paid on a set schedule. With installment loans you should follow the 10% rule. One payment should not be more than 10% of your monthly net income. For example, if you have a net income of $2,400 a month, no one payment in this category should be more than $240. If at all possible, the total amount of your credit card payments shouldn't equal more than the 10% rule. As previously stated cash flow is the most important factor in your money plan, so it is important to spread payments out. You can ask for different due dates that will work best with your cash flow.

Fixed Expenses

This section represents your fixed bill payments like your cell phone, cable TV and Internet, insurance premiums and household utilities. Some of these payments are unavoidable like utilities; however, some of these payments are negotiable. Always shop around for the best deals on all these bills. There could be savings with all your plans, especially with your cable, Internet and cell phone. Also, be aware of the fees charged by counties and municipalities for water and garbage collection.

Spending Money

This section is for cash purchases you make during the month. From groceries and transportation costs to spending money on entertainment and miscellaneous items, this is the money that always seems to get away from you during the month. You should withdraw cash from your account when you get paid that way you can keep an account of how this money is spent. And know once the cash is gone you can no longer buy coffee, in the morning or go out to eat. This is a helpful way to stay within your money plan.

The following chart is an example of a money plan for someone whose annual salary is $39,000 and is paid bi-weekly.

Note: The federal, state and local taxes as well as the medical and dental deductions may vary depending on your city and state.

January Money Plan

Income	1/8/2016	1/22/2016	
Gross Income	**$1,500.00**	**$1,500.00**	**$3,000.00**

Taxes	1/8/2016	1/22/2016
Federal 8.5%	$122.40	$122.40
Medicare 1.45%	$21.75	$21.75
Social Security 6.2%	$93.00	$93.00
State Tax 2.5%	$37.50	$37.50
Local Tax 2%	$30.00	$30.00
State Unemp. Ins. .07%	$1.05	$1.05
Total	$305.70	$305.70

Deductions	1/8/2016	1/22/2016
401k Pre-Tax 3%	$45.00	$45.00
Dental	$6.19	$6.19
Medical	$30.37	$30.37
Total	$81.56	$81.56

Net Income	$1,112.74	$1,112.74	$2,225.48

Savings	1/8/16	1/22/16	
ME Fund	$25.00	$25.00	
SAFE Fund	$40.00	$40.00	
Total	$65.00	$65.00	**$130.00**

Credit Expenses	1/8/16	1/22/16	Total
Mortgage	$330.00	$330.00	$660.00
Student Loan		$160.00	$160.00
Car Loan	$110.00	$110.00	$220.00
Credit Card #1	$30.00		$30.00
Credit Card #2	$30.00		$30.00
Total	$500.00	$600.00	**$1,100.00**

Fixed Expenses	**1/8/16**	**1/22/16**	Total
Life Insurance	$40.00		$40.00
Car Insurance		$175.00	$175.00
Cable Internet	$80.00		$80.00
Cell Phone	$80.00		$80.00
Electric & Gas		$90.00	$90.00
Water	$35.00		$35.00
Netflix	$16.40		$16.40
Total	$251.40	$265.00	$516.40

Total	**$816.40**	**$930.00**	**$1,746.40**

Spending Money	**$296.34**	**$182.74**	**$479.08**

With $479.08 left in your plan you have some decisions to make.

With this money you still have to grocery shop and put gas in your car as well as buy lunch and take care of all your personal needs. Using this money wisely requires you to create a balance with the things you want, using the money you have. If this money runs out before the end of the month it is important to remember that there is money in your ME Fund that can be used and that using your credit card should always be a last resort, if at all.

Money Plan Tips

There are many ways to keep track of your money plan including an Excel worksheet on your computer or by writing it down on sheets of paper. There is a sample of a blank money plan in the back of this book.

One option to prevent you from missing the due date of your bills is to put them on auto pay. If your payment is under $50, like a credit card, a life insurance policy or Netflix, you can have the payments taken directly out of your checking every month. $50 is a small enough amount to always keep in your checking account to cover the payment and also avoid an overdraft fee. Remember; set the payments for the day after you are scheduled to receive your paycheck, in the event your paycheck is delayed.

The biggest reason your money plan could be thrown off is if you buy lunch and coffee everyday. Lunch and morning coffee are daily expenses that are small, but add up over the course of a month. Buying delicious sandwiches and coffee has a place in society; they are easy and convenient to buy instead of bringing them from home. The problem is when you want one of these items everyday. If you maintain a balance with these items, by spacing out your enjoyment of them, you will have the money you need every month. Remember; try not to use your debit card for these purchases.

What are the bills you can cut back on in the plan to save money? In the categories of credit and fixed expenses, there is always a possibility to call the creditor and negotiate a lower amount. You can also cancel optional services all together like magazine subscriptions and your cable/internet package.

However, the best option you have to put more money into your plan is to eliminate debt.

The DRIP Method

Becoming debt free may be the most difficult part of your personal finance journey and there are many methods and techniques to help you reach this goal. On this journey you are also trying to maintain a decent credit score. To achieve both of these goals, the best method to eliminate debt and improve your credit score is to use the Debt Reducing Interest Plan (DRIP). This is a plan designed to have you put any extra money you have on your highest interest credit card, while making the minimum payment on the remaining bills under the credit expense category. When that credit card is paid off, take that payment and apply it to the next highest interest credit card. Make sure you keep the paid off credit card account open; it will continue to contribute to your credit history. Continue this pattern until all your debt is paid off.

The following chart displays the payments, balances and interest rates of the bills from the previous example. Pay your highest interest card credit card first with any extra cash you may have to put towards this bill.

Credit Expenses	Payments	Balance	Interest
Credit Card #1	$30.00	$2,000.00	12.90%
Credit Card #2	$30.00	$1,000.00	12.00%
Car Loan	$220.00	$15,000.00	13.00%
Mortgage	$660.00	$115,000.00	5.00%
Student Loan	$160.00	$17,000.00	4.00%
Total	$1,100.00	$150,000.00	

Credit card #1 has the highest credit card interest rate; start paying down this account first. Even though the car loan interest rate is the highest overall interest rate, it is better to pay the credit card to reduce the total cost of your debt and improve your credit score over time. When choosing between an installment loan and a credit card account to apply extra payments, choose the credit card because it has a bigger impact on your credit score. Credit cards prove you are a good manager of your credit and installment loans prove you are responsible to make payments on time.

Remember, when credit card #1 is paid off, the $30 payment will be applied to credit card #2 making the new payment $60 plus any extra money you have to apply to the payment. This is a long-range plan, it will take some time to pay these debts off, but with determination and discipline you can do it.

Another popular debt reduction method is to pay the lowest balance credit account, regardless of the interest rate. This builds confidence and a feeling of accomplishment. Whatever method works for you, just make extra payments to eliminate debt quicker.

America has determined that having debt is a character-defining trait and paying it off is a sign you are a good person. This thinking makes paying down debt an emotional endeavor. You need debt to improve your life, but remember to make on time payments and you will be on track to payoff the debt and maintaining your good name.

A money plan is more than just words and numbers on a page. It is a picture of the reality of your current lifestyle. The conflict arises when you try to live beyond your income. Create a plan for the year or at least for a six-month time frame. This way you will have an idea of what to expect.

When an interruption occurs in your plan, due to overspending or an unexpected expense, whether the expense is small or large, is one of the top reasons why people give up on the plan. Once you are off track it is easy to abandon the whole idea of a money plan. The problem is, you are still earning money and bills are still due and without a plan, you are a rudderless ship on the sea of personal finance. It cannot be overemphasized that maintaining your money plan will keep you on track to successfully manage your financial life.

Finding the balance with your income and your expectations is the key to sticking with your money plan. Ultimately, the money plan will allow you to have peace of mind while living within your income.

The Summary

This book has explored eight pillars of personal finance, which represent the foundation for a good financial life. Saving, retirement, credit, loans, home buying, insurance, banking and budgeting, are the pathway to finding success on your journey. These building blocks affect your future needs and your ability to manage money.

The purchases and transactions you make along your financial journey are all your choices, whether it is a credit card, car, education or a house, they are a part of your financial life. A ME Fund, a SAFE Fund and saving for retirement are also elements in that life. The key is to find balance with them all.

On a basic level your financial life comes down to savings, managing credit, and controlling spending. These are the guidelines you must master on your journey. The financial decisions you make when you are building your life end up being the bills you have in your life. So, make good decisions.

GLOSSARY

401(k) – a tax deferred defined contribution retirement plan offered by companies. Employees make contributions through payroll deductions. These contributions are a fixed amount or percentage of their income.

403(b) – a tax deferred defined contribution retirement plan for employees of charitable and non-profit organizations, including educational institutions to which employees make contributions through payroll deductions. These contributions are a fixed amount or percentage of their income.

4% Rule – a rule of thumb used to determine the amount of money to withdraw each year from retirement accounts.

12b-1 Fee – an annual marketing or distribution fee on a mutual fund. The 12b-1 is considered to be an operational expense and is included in a fund's expense ratio.

Annual Percentage Rate (APR) – the annual interest rate charged for borrowing money from a lender or earning money through an investment. It is expressed as a percentage that represents the actual yearly cost of funds over the term of a loan or the return on an investment.

Annual Percentage Yield (APY) – the effective annual rate of return on an investment, taking into account the effect of compound interest. It is also the effective cost of a loan including compound interest.

Appraisal – a valuation of a property for a real estate transaction by an authorized person. This estimate is used to determine the possible selling price for the property.

Asset – a property that has monetary value, including personal possessions such as a house, car, savings and investments.

Authorized User – a person, who has permission to use and/or carry another person's credit card and benefit from the credit history of the credit card, but isn't legally responsible for paying the bill.

Glossary

Blended Mutual Fund – a mutual fund that buys a combination of stock and bonds to provide both income and capital appreciation while attempting to avoid excessive risk.

Beneficiary – the person or organization designated to receive the funds or other property from a trust, insurance policy or retirement account.

Bonds – an investment in which an investor loans money to an entity, which is borrowing the funds for a defined period of time at a variable or fixed interest rate.

Bond Mutual Fund – a mutual fund that invests primarily in bonds, typically corporate, municipal or U.S. government bonds.

Capital Gains – the profit an investor receives when he or she sells an investment for more than the purchase price.

Certificate of Deposit (CD) – a savings certificate with a fixed maturity date, specified fixed interest rate that can be issued in any amount of money.

Closing Costs – expenses over and above the price of the property in a real estate transaction. Costs incurred include loan origination fees, discount points, appraisal fee, title searches, title insurance, surveys, deed recording fees, and credit report charges.

Compound Interest – interest calculated on the initial principal and also the accumulated interest of a deposit or loan.

Credit Limit – the maximum amount of credit a financial institution extends to a customer through a line of credit as well as the maximum amount a credit card company allows a borrower to spend on a single card.

Credit Report – a detailed report of an individual's credit history.

Credit Score – a statistical number that determines a person's creditworthiness based on the information in their credit report.

Glossary

Credit Utilization Ratio – the percentage of a consumer's available credit that has been used.

Direct Deposit – a person's paycheck is electronically deposited into a financial institution or pre paid debit card.

Dividend – the distribution of a portion of a company's profits declared by a company's board of directors and paid to shareholders.

Free Application for Federal Student Aid (FAFSA) – the form that must be filled out to qualify for federal financial aid for higher education.

Federal Deposit Insurance Corporation (FDIC) – a U.S. government agency that insures cash deposits, including certificates of deposit, that have been opened in member institutions, for up to $250,000 for each account type.

Growth Mutual Fund – a stock mutual fund that seeks long-term capital appreciation. Growth funds generally purchase common stocks of companies that advisors believe have long-term growth potential.

Hardship Distribution – a distribution from a retirement plan prior to age 59½ based on a qualified need such as a medical expense. Hardship distributions are subject to income tax, as well as a 10% penalty.

Index – a statistical composite that measures changes in the financial markets. Well known market indices include the S&P 500 Index, the Dow 30 and the Nasdaq 100 Composite Index.

Index Mutual Fund – a mutual fund that seeks to track the performance of a stock index by investing in the stocks that comprise that index.

Individual Retirement Account (IRA) – a self-funded, tax deferred retirement account, established by an individual, not by an employer. The contributions may be subject to tax deductions on the account holder's federal tax return, often referred to as a traditional IRA.

Interest – the charge for the privilege of borrowing money. It is also the rate that is paid on the principle of an investment.

Glossary

Judgment – a court order to the loser of a lawsuit to pay the winner a specified sum of money.

Large Cap Mutual Fund – a mutual fund that invests primarily in stocks of large American companies or companies with a market capitalization that exceeds $10 Billion.

Liability – a financial obligation, for example, a mortgage or credit card debt; the opposite of an asset.

ME Fund - stands for "My Everything", this is the money that you spend on things that bring you happiness, whether it's an item or an experience with friends or family.

Money Market Mutual Fund – an investment whose objective is to earn interest for shareholders while maintaining a net asset value (NAV) of $1 per share.

Mortgage – a long-term loan used to finance the purchase of real estate, as the borrower, or mortgager, you repay the lender, or mortgagee, the loan principle plus interest, gradually building your equity in the property.

Mutual Fund – an investment vehicle made up of a pool of funds collected from many investors for the purpose of investing in securities such as stocks, bonds and money market instruments. Portfolio managers, who invest the fund's money and attempt to produce capital gains and income for the fund's investors, operate mutual funds.

National Credit Union Administration (NCUA) – an agency of the U.S. federal government that insures cash deposits, including certificates of deposit, that have been opened in member institutions, for up to $250,000 for each account type for federal credit unions.

Net Asset Value (NAV) – the value per share of a mutual fund on a specific date or time. The share per dollar amount of the fund is based on the total value of all the securities in its portfolio divided by the total number of shares outstanding.

Glossary

Origination Fee – an up-front fee charged by a lender for processing a new loan application. This fee is compensation for putting the loan in place.

Portfolio – a grouping of financial assets such as stocks, bonds and cash equivalents.

Principle – the amount of money that is financed, borrowed or invested.

Rollover IRA – a transfer of funds from a retirement account such as a 401(k) or 403(b) into a traditional IRA or a Roth IRA.

Roth IRA – an individual retirement plan that bears many similarities to the traditional IRA. The biggest distinction between the two is how they're taxed. Roth IRAs are funded with after-tax dollars; the contributions are not tax deductible.

Standard & Poor's 500 Index – an index of 500 stocks seen as a leading indicator of U.S. equities and a reflection of the performance of the overall U.S. economy.

SAFE Fund – stands for "Saving Amounts For Emergencies", also known as an emergency fund, will provide a financial cushion in the event a crisis or an unforeseen circumstance presents itself.

Stock – a security that represent an ownership interest in a company.

Tax Deduction – a reduction in tax obligation from a taxpayer's gross income on the annual federal tax return.

Tax Deferred – a status that refers to investment earnings such as interest. Dividends or capital gains that accumulate tax-free until the investor takes the gains out of the account.

Tax-Free – certain types of financial products that are not taxed and the earnings are also not taxed.

Term Life Insurance – a policy with a set age limit on the coverage period.

Title – a bundle of rights in a piece of property in which a party may own either a legal interest or equitable interest.

Title Search – an examination of public records to determine and confirm a property's legal ownership and to find out what claims are on the property.

Title Insurance – an insurance policy that covers the loss of ownership interest in a property due to legal defects and is required if the property is under mortgage.

U. S. Treasury – the government department responsible for issuing all Treasury bonds, notes and bills, they are considered one of the safest investments in the world.

Universal Life Insurance – a type of flexible permanent life insurance offering a savings element, like Whole life insurance, which is invested to provide cash value buildup. Universal life insurance allows the policyholder to use the interest from the accumulated savings to help pay the premiums over time.

Value Mutual Fund – a stock mutual fund that primarily invests in stocks that is determined to be undervalue in price and that are likely to pay dividends.

W-2 Forms – the form that an employer must send an employee and the Internal Revenue Service at the end of the year, stating all earnings and taxes.

W-4 Form – an employee completes this form to indicate their tax status to the employer.

Whole Life Insurance – a type of life insurance that provides insurance coverage for the contract holders for their entire life. Unlike term life insurance, which covers the contract holder until a specified age limit, a whole life policy never runs out as long as you make the premium payments.

RESOURCES

Annualcreditreport.com – The official website for obtaining your free credit report from the three credit bureaus: Equifax, Experian and Transunion. You are entitled to one free report from each credit bureau every 12 months.

Bankrate.com – This is a great website for interest rate information on saving and all types of loans, they also have calculators for every part of your financial life.

CNNmoney.com – A good personal finance information website and financial news of the day.

Consumerfinance.gov – The Consumer Financial Protection Bureau is a government website, that provides personal finance information and consumer protection from companies that commit fraud.

Dailypf.com – A little self-promotion, check out my website. I provide daily updates about personal finance news and tips.

Edmunds.com – Edmunds is a trusted resource to use when you are researching the value of a new or used car.

Equifax.com – One of the three major credit-reporting bureaus. The other two are Experian and Transunion.

Experian.com – One of the three major credit-reporting agencies. The other two are Equifax and Transunion.

Findabetterbank.com – This website allows you to compare checking account fees and features for banks in your area.

IRS.gov – Internal Revenue Service is the government agency that collects taxes from American citizens and businesses.

RESOURCES

Kbb.com – Kelley Blue Book is a great website to research the value of a new or used car.

Mint.com – This website offers useful tools and tips for personal finance.

Myfico.com – The official website for obtaining your FICO score. The leading credit scores most lenders use to determine credit worthiness.

SSA.gov – The official website for the social security administration.

Studentaid.ed.gov – A website sponsored by the U.S. Department of Education that provides financial aid information for post secondary education.

Transunion.com – One of the three major credit-reporting bureaus. The other two are Experian and Equifax.

MONEY PLAN SAMPLE WORKSHEETS

Income	Date	Date	
Gross Income			

Taxes	Date	Date	
Federal 8.5%			
Medicare 1.45%			
Social Security 6.2%			
State Tax 2.5%			
Local Tax 2%			
State Unemp. Ins .07%			
Total	$0.00	$0.00	

Deductions	Date	Date	
401k Pre-Tax 3%			
Dental			
Medical			
Total			

Net Income			

Savings	Date	Date	
ME Fund			
SAFE Fund			
Total			

Credit Expenses	Date	Date	Total
Mortgage			
Student Loan			
Car Loan			
Credit Card #1			
Credit Card #2			
Total			

Fixed Expenses	Date	Date	Total
Life Insurance			
Car Insurance			
Cable Internet			
Cell Phone			
Electric & Gas			
Water			
Netflix			
Total			

Total

Spending Money

DRIP Method

Credit Expenses	Payments	Balance	Interest
Mortgage			
Student Loan			
Car Loan			
Credit Card #1			
Credit Card #2			
Total			

CREDIT REPAIR LETTERS

The following are the steps to filing a dispute with the three credit reporting agencies and sample letters to send for each kind of dispute. In your letter, clearly identify each mistake, state the facts, explain why you are disputing the information and request it to be removed or corrected.

Steps to filing a dispute
Write a letter to the credit agency that sent you the report.
Provide the account number for the accounts you think are not accurate.
For each account, explain concisely why you believe it is not accurate.
If at all possible, include copies of bills, cleared checks or money order stubs that show you have paid these accounts on time.
Provide your address and telephone number at the end of the letter so the credit agency can contact you for more information, if necessary.
Make a copy of your letter and all supporting documents before you send them to the credit agency.
Send the letter and all the supporting documents, if there are any. You may choose to use Certified Mail with a Return Receipt to have proof of when the letter was received. The consumer reporting agency or the creditor generally has 30-45 days to investigate your claim.

Removing inaccurate information from your credit report.

Date

Your Name
Your Address

Credit Bureau Name
Credit Bureau Address

To Whom It May Concern:

This letter is a formal complaint that you are reporting inaccurate credit information on my credit report. I have circled the item(s) I am disputing on the attached copy of the report I received.

I am writing to have this incorrect information removed from my credit report, due to its damaging effects on my credit standing. *The following account information is inaccurate for the following reason(s)_____.*

This information needs to be verified and deleted from my credit report as soon as possible:

Creditor Company – Account #34523467

Sincerely,

Your Signature

Your Name
Your Social Security number
Optional: Include any supporting documents.

Requesting a credit report after you are denied credit.

Date

Your Name
Your Address

Credit Bureau Name
Credit Bureau Address

To Whom It May Concern:

I have recently been denied an application for [credit card or loan] and, I do not have a credit report to validate my credit profile. I am requesting a copy of my credit report. In accordance with the Fair Credit Reporting Act, I have the right to request a free copy of my credit report. My personal information is as follows:

Full Name:
Date of Birth:
Social Security Number:
Current address:
Former address (If current address is less than 2 years)

I am enclosing a copy of the credit denial letter, a photocopy of my driver's license as proof of my current address and a copy my Social Security card. Please send me a copy of my credit report as soon as possible.

Sincerely,

Your Signature

Your Name

Request to remove an inquiry from a your credit report.

Date

Your Name
Your Address

Credit Bureau Name
Credit Bureau Address

To Whom It May Concern:

This letter is to bring to your attention that my credit report reflects an inquiry from your company that I did not approve. You are not legally entitled to access my credit report without my authorization. Therefore, I request that you delete this inquiry from my credit report immediately, because this inquiry will affect my chances of getting new credit.

Please forward me a written document stating that you have accepted my proposal to delete this unauthorized inquiry.

Sincerely,

Your Signature

Your Name

ABOUT THE AUTHOR

Mkemo London is passionate about learning and teaching financial literacy. He has made it his life's mission to educate people about the topics of personal finance. He has been a speaker at churches and non-profits throughout the Philadelphia area. He is the editor and founder of the personal finance website dailypf.com. He is the author of *Building Wealth with $50: the 50 Best Dividend Stocks to Buy without a Broker.*

A native of Philadelphia, PA, Mr. London holds a Bachelor of Science in Business Administration in Management from Thomas Edison State University. He is also a United States Navy veteran and resides in New Jersey with his wife.

www.ingramcontent.com/pod-product-compliance
Lightning Source LLC
Chambersburg PA
CBHW051542170526
45165CB00002B/839